THE MICHELIN BUILDING

Published to celebrate the reopening

The Directors of the
Michelin Tyre Co. Ltd.
have the honour to invite

to the opening of their
new premises, 81 Fulham Road,
Chelsea, London, S.W.
at 12 o'clock noon on Friday,
20th January, 1911.

Edward Manville, Esq.
President of the Society of
Motor Manufacturers & Traders,
has kindly consented to officiate

R.S.V.P.

Compiled and written by WENDY HITCHMOUGH

CONRAN OCTOPUS • HEINEMANN

We would like to thank the Michelin Tyre Company, Monsieur François Michelin and all his staff for their great help and support given to our architects and designers in the refurbishment of the building.

Terence Conran and Paul Hamlyn

First published in 1987 jointly by

Conran Octopus Limited
37 Shelton Street
London WC2H 9HN

William Heinemann Ltd
10 Upper Grosvenor Street,
London W1X 9PA

ISBN: 0 434 39840 3

Printed in England

Previous page: Michelin's original invitation to the opening of the building in January 1911.
Following page: The Michelin Building in 1987, just before it reopened.

Above: the frontispiece for Burmantofts' 1911 catalogue shows the building in use with mechanics at work changing tyres in the drive-in tyre fitting bay. Burmantofts, a part of the Leeds Fire Clay Company, used the Michelin Building to promote the virtues of their new and relatively untested 'Marmo' facing tiles.

CONTENTS

The Michelin Building has always been an important part of my enjoyment of London. Its sheer ebullience seems to personify the carefree world that existed before the First World War when innovation and entrepreneurialism were so readily accepted. The Michelin brothers were symbolic of the spirit of the age with their amazing foresight of how the world would develop.

When I started Habitat in 1964 in a dull 60's building alongside Michelin, I used to look avariciously across at it and think how wonderful it would be if one day they decided that they no longer needed it as a tyre depot. Suddenly about two years ago, the property world was inflamed with the news that Michelin was prepared to sell the building.

Now, my friend Paul Hamlyn and his wife loved the building just as much as I did and he also happened to be looking for new offices for his burgeoning publishing business. I wanted a bigger space for our highly successful Conran Shop and we both wanted to open a restaurant. There was enormous competition for this wonderful building, but probably the thing that clinched the deal for us was Michelin's conviction that we would do everything possible to restore the building immaculately and that it would house activities sympathetic to the ideals of the Michelin brothers, i.e. design, marketing, publishing, food and wine.

This book will tell you everything about the long, complex and costly process of the conversion of the building to contemporary standards. It may also cause you to wonder if an ebullient building such as this was designed today would it stand a chance of getting planning permission, and if not, why not?

TERENCE CONRAN

I have always loved the Michelin Building, both as a classic example of the finest features of the architecture of the time and as a building with tremendous personality. But my excitement when it came on the market was for another reason too: its potential as office space for the expanding Octopus Publishing Group.

I believe that publishers need surroundings which are both visually exciting and complementary to the fluid creative nature of their work. I also believe that imaginative and responsible development of office space is one way in which a business or company can give a great deal to its neighbourhood. From both perspectives, the Michelin Building was a unique opportunity.

Since that first excitement, two and a half years of planning, restoration and refurbishment have passed. It has been a privilege and a pleasure to be involved in that work in some small way, the pleasure being greatly enhanced by my partnership with Terence Conran.

I hope that in the future, as in the past, the building will stand for excellence in all its associations — design, publishing, food and wine. More simply, but equally important, I hope that the redefinition of the role of the building will allow more people to use it and so to enjoy its wonderful architecture and design.

PAUL HAMLYN

INTRODUCTION

The Michelin Building, commissioned by the Michelin Tyre Company Ltd. as their first permanent British headquarters in 1909, has been a favourite London landmark for many years. Its exuberant stylistic individualism has been variously described as an example of Art Nouveau, proto-Art Deco, Secessionist Functionalism and geometrical Classicism. It has even been described as 'the most completely French of any Edwardian building in London'. In fact it defies definition as an example of any rigid architectural style. Designed by an employee of the company, probably under the guidance of Edouard and André Michelin, it owes more to the imagination, vivacity and outrageously irreverent flair for public relations of these two men than to any notion of the architectural taste of its time.

In 1985 Michelin moved out of the building after seventy-five years of continuous occupancy and in June of that year it was bought by Sir Terence Conran and Paul Hamlyn. Planning permission for a restaurant, bar, major retail store and additional office space was obtained and a programme of extensive restoration was begun. The refurbishment of the building and reinstatement of many of its most prominent original features has given the building both a new vitality and a new role for the future while retaining its original character.

The Michelin Building, also known as Michelin House, reflects not only the ambitions and aspirations of the Michelin Company but also a turning point in the history of early motoring. Indeed, the two are inextricably linked. By 1911, the year in which the Michelin Building opened, motoring in Britain was already popular, prestigious and highly respectable. But this was also a time when new speed records were being made and broken with an almost total disregard for personal safety; when long-distance races like the 1907 Peking to Paris excited the imaginations of motorists across the world. It is these pioneer races and long-distance challenges, won on Michelin tyres, that are shown on the tiled picture panels around the outside and in the entrance hall of the building. And it is the excitement of breaking the speed limit with inadequate brakes on unmade roads that the building exploits.

It is against the background of the history of Michelin House, seen in the context of the early days of motoring and the character then of the Michelin Company, that the most recent extensions and developments of the building should be seen.

Below: The Hon. Evelyn Ellis in his Panhard Levassor car at the first British motor demonstration in 1895.

Right: The perils of steam conquered, one of the earliest attempts at 'horseless' public transport was Gurney's Steam Carriage of 1827.

The emergence of a French company, Michelin, as one of the leading suppliers of pneumatic tyres in Britain perfectly reflected the difference in attitudes to early motoring on the Continent and in Britain. For although Britain was the richest, the most powerful and the most industrially advanced nation in the world in the mid-nineteenth century, her attitude towards motoring was conservative in the extreme. From the outset the landowning gentry, still the power behind the government, were against the early steam carriages – naturally, since they had financial interests in horse-drawn carriages and the new-comers to the road represented potential competition in transporting both goods and people. Quite aside from that, they created clouds of dust, chaos, and were a terrifying hazard to every horse they passed.

Landowners were able to levy prohibitive tolls on steam carriages wishing to cross their land but, far more effectively, the Locomotive Act of 1865 crippled the development of the motor car in Britain by specifying that:

Firstly, at least three persons shall be employed to drive or conduct such Locomotive, and if more than two waggons or carriages be attached thereto, an additional person shall be employed who shall take charge of such waggons or carriages. . . . Secondly, one of such persons, while such Locomotive is in motion, shall precede such Locomotive on foot by not less than sixty yards and shall carry a red flag constantly displayed, and shall

Right: The catalogue of the first British motor show of 1896 is reassuringly romantic and conservative in style, playing down the excitement and aggressive modernity of the new motor vehicles.

warn drivers or horses and riders of the approach of such Locomotive and shall signal the driver thereof when it is necessary to stop and shall assist horses, and carriages drawn by horses, passing the same.

The new speed limits of two miles per hour in built-up areas and four miles per hour in the countryside confined the use of the motor car in Britain to a leisurely pastime for the idle rich. The law, which became known as the 'Red Flag Act', was not repealed altogether, until 1896.

It was in France and Germany, where potential market conditions were more favourable, that the first prototypes for petrol driven cars were developed. Karl Benz and Gottlieb Daimler built the first commercially viable petrol driven vehicles in 1884 and 1885; Emile Levassor's Panhard Levassor of 1891 established the layout which remains valid today for the radiator, engine, clutch, gearbox, transmission and rear axle (in that order), thus transforming the appearance of motor vehicles. This model of Panhard Levassor was the second petrol driven car to be imported into England (the first being an 1888 Benz). On 15 October 1895 it was driven with three other vehicles to Tunbridge Wells for the first motor demonstration.

The demonstration formed part of a campaign to introduce the motor car to Britain. It was led by Frederick Simms and a small number of enthusiasts who hoped that by informing the public of the value of the new vehicles they might persuade Parliament to remove the restrictions of the Red Flag Act. In the same year Simms and his associates founded *The Autocar*, the first motoring magazine, and between 9 May and 8 August 1896 they organised the first British motor show at the Imperial Institute in London. Members of Parliament were invited to the show where demonstrations of the new 'horseless carriages' were given and the future King Edward VII, then the Prince of Wales, was given a drive in a belt-driven Daimler car.

The campaign was successful. A few months later, on 14 November, the Light (Road) Locomotives Act raised the national speed limit to twelve and fourteen miles per hour and revoked the clause requiring a pedestrian to walk ahead of the vehicle. Britain was ready to move forward into a new age of motoring and a celebratory 'Emancipation Day' run from London to Brighton was arranged. Thirty-five vehicles set off for Brighton. Before the start a symbolic red flag was ceremonially torn up. In spite of poor weather and a fatal accident involving a pedestrian, twenty-two vehicles completed the drive – although some of these made at least part of the journey by train!

From this point the British market was quick to develop and expand and by the beginning of the twentieth century it represented one of the largest markets in the world for motoring goods. Nevertheless, because the French and the Germans had been the first to design and produce the early motor cars, it was their vehicles and accessories that were imported into Britain to meet the new demand.

Above: 'They start out feeling bright and gay. To drive to Brighton all the way.' The 1896 London to Brighton run is still celebrated today.

The invention of the pneumatic tyre, which enabled lighter, faster and smoother cars to be built, was a development fundamental to the history of early motoring. Before that cars ran on solid rubber tyres or on steel rims and, since a vehicle could weigh up to four tons with little suspension, they gave a very uncomfortable ride on the uneven road surfaces, even at slow speeds. Sturdier cars were built to withstand the vibrations, but the increase in weight corresponded to a comparable reduction in speed and put even more strain on already inadequate braking and steering systems.

The first pneumatic tyre was invented by R.W. Thomson, who took out a patent for an 'aerial wheel' in 1845. The Thomson tyre was intended to 'lessen the power required to draw carriages, making their motion easier and diminishing the noise they make ...'. Successful demonstrations were carried out in Regent's Park, but the tyre was not commercially developed and seems to have been forgotten until J.B. Dunlop reinvented the pneumatic tyre for the bicycle in 1888. Dunlop was a Scottish veterinary surgeon working in Belfast and his first pneumatic tyre was made for his son's bicycle. Cycling in Britain was very much in vogue in the 1880s and the pneumatic tyre soon caught on. The new tyres were faster and smoother, although they also punctured easily. Intrepid cyclists toured the countryside, abroad as well as at home, and as early as 1889 bicycles on Dunlop tyres were finding their way into France. One cyclist in need of a repair was brought into a rubber-making factory at Clermont-Ferrand run by Edouard and André Michelin. The tyre, which was glued on to the rim, took three hours to remove, repair, stick back and restitch, and then it had to be left overnight to dry. The following morning Edouard Michelin tried the bicycle out around the factory yard. The repair failed after only a hundred yards or so. But Edouard is reputed to have written to his brother André in Paris:

> *Riding on air is wonderful, but the stuck-on tyre is useless. As long as it takes a day to repair a puncture, this new tyre will never be a success. It has to be made easy to remove and then it will give the bicycle a new future.*

The two brothers set to work to design a detachable pneumatic tyre and in 1891 they took out their first patent. The Michelin tyre consisted of an air-filled tube that was completely separate from its cover. Each edge of the cover finished in a bead that was locked between the rim and a steel ring-shaped strip. No more glueing or stitching. By taking out seventeen bolts the rim could be removed and the tyre dismantled and refitted in fifteen minutes. The new Michelin detachable pneumatic would still puncture with alarming regularity, but the advantages of the speed with which it could be removed and replaced more than compensated for its drawbacks.

Before the tyre could be put into production the newspaper *Petit Journal* organised a cycle race from Paris to Brest and back. Most of the 210 competitors had entered their bicycles on solid tyres, with a few on Dunlop pneumatics. The Michelin brothers

were to use the race to promote their new invention. The favourite, Laval, had already signed up to ride on Dunlop tyres so the brothers approached Charles Terront, a famous racing cyclist who had come out of retirement for the event. Only a few days before the race and with just one set of pneumatic tyres ready to use, André and Edouard Michelin persuaded Terront to try out the new detachable tyres. To his manager's fury Terront returned from his trial run filled with enthusiasm for the tyres and agreed to use them in the race.

It was the first long-distance race of its kind and crowds of spectators gathered at the start. Terront set off amidst hoots of ridicule. The new tyres with their clumsy looking bolts did not inspire confidence in his supporters and he had five punctures on the outward leg of the journey. By the time he reached Brest he was a full hour and a half behind Laval, but the favourite was exhausted. Laval went to bed and Terront slipped through the back streets of the town, clocking in at the checkpoint without Laval knowing about it. Then Laval had a puncture on the return journey to Paris. Terront won the race with a full eight hour lead and a complete day in front of the rider in third place. It had taken Terront three days and nights, without a moment's sleep, to ride 750 miles at an average speed of ten miles per hour. But the achievement was not only one of supreme athletic endurance. It was the first racing victory for Michelin tyres.

Orders began to pour in. Michelin's entire stock of detachable pneumatic tyres at the

PARIS-BORDEAUX 1895

1ERE VOITURE sur PNEUS MICHELIN

Above: The Michelin brothers themselves drove the first car to run on pneumatic tyres in an eventful race from Paris to Bordeaux and back in 1895. Although the tiled picture gives an indication of speed that the photograph could not, the portraits of Edouard and André are still rigid with concentrtion.

end of the race amounted to twelve tyres, with an output of not more than ten per day, but the brothers continued to improve and develop both their pneumatic tyres and their production. Soon the tyres were in demand in England as well as France. Less than two years later, the Michelin representative at the 1893 Stanley Show in London was able to demonstrate that the latest Michelin inner tube could be replaced in under two minutes; he collected orders for four thousand tyres. The brothers continued to concentrate their resources on developing better tyres at more competitive prices, announcing their first small price reduction, to £3 10s 0d for one bicycle tyre, in 1894. This policy, combined with aggressive advertising techniques and the exploitation of long-distance cycle races to demonstrate their latest products, led to the rapid growth of the company.

Then André and Edouard Michelin began to turn their attention towards tyres for motor cars. In 1894 the first competitive motor car race was run from Paris to Rouen. André Michelin was a passenger in Léon Serpolet's car and the experience convinced him that motoring could only succeed on pneumatic tyres. There were about 200 cars in the whole of France at the time so the design and production of a new tyre was hardly financially viable. Nevertheless, André's conviction that the way forward into the twentieth century would be by car and on Michelin tyres led the brothers to develop a prototype.

The first city to city car races were attracting terrific interest and publicity at

that time and Edouard and André wanted to make use of the 1895 Paris-Bordeaux race to promote their new invention, just as they had done with the cycle tyres. However, their faith in the potential of the pneumatic was not shared by the major motor car manufacturers: not one of them would run the risk of entering their cars on completely untried tyres, especially ones filled with air which were quite likely to burst. But the brothers were determined. They entered the three company vehicles that they had built themselves, all of which ran on pneumatic tyres.

Forty-six cars began the 750 mile race from Paris to Bordeaux and back. The Michelin brothers were driving L'Eclair (Lightning) a vehicle that owed its name to its reputation for steering a zig-zag course rather than for any claim to speed. Even before they were out of Paris L'Eclair was in trouble; somebody had put water into the petrol tank by mistake, causing the engine to stall. The average speed from Paris to Orléans was only six miles per hour, increasing to nine miles per hour on the stretch to Angoulême. The tyres punctured after the first hundred miles, but they were changed in a record half an hour. The steel wheel spokes kept breaking and finally had to be replaced in their entirety. By the time the brothers reached Bordeaux, the leading car had already left thirty-eight hours before.

On the return drive to Paris both the second and third gears gave up so that it was necessary to wait for a downhill stretch before changing from first gear straight into ourth. At Tours André and Edouard were told that they had been disqualified for changing the wheel spokes, but they were determined to complete the race. At Blois they forgot to put out the burners before filling up with petrol and fire extinguishers had to be called for to put out the flames; closer to Paris another fire broke out when red hot cylinders melted the solder around the carburettor and the petrol burst into flames. A dilapidated L'Eclair finally reached Paris, one of only nine cars to complete the race. The next day the Michelin brothers were able to boast to the press that their new pneumatic tyres had run the full 750 miles of the race.

Even this impressive achievement left many motor manufacturers wary of the Michelin pneumatic tyres as standard fittings to their new vehicles. They could not be convinced that the average motorist would be willing to take on such a radical new invention – or its additional expense. It is another example of André's and Edouard's supreme confidence in their product that they offered to buy De Dion's and Léon Bollée's entire output for six months so that the cars could be retailed with pneumatic tyres. The gamble paid off and although pneumatic tyres were perhaps the most tiresome and expensive component of motoring in the nineties, their advantages in increased speed and smoothness and the lighter structures that they facilitated far out-weighed their drawbacks. Michelin pneumatics were soon the standard new tyre on most of the cars in France. At the same time, a new market was opening up on the other side of the Channel.

PARIS-BREST
1891

CH. TERRONT

Above: The pictures shown on the tiles around the outside and in the entrance of the Michelin Building were often based on photographs. Here Charles Terront is shown riding in the 1891 Paris to Brest cycle race on the first Michelin pneumatic tyres.

By 1905, just ten years after the famous Paris-Bordeaux race, the Michelin Company Ltd. was planning a new headquarters in Paris and a small branch was already established in Britain. The British had by this time taken to the new mode of transport with immense enthusiasm.

The early motoring press give us a good indication of the sorts of people who owned the first motor cars, their interests and preoccupations. One of the earliest editions of *The Car* shows King Edward VII on the cover; inside there are articles on stately homes and golf courses, presumably that one might have driven to, together with portraits of celebrated society ladies and advertisements for the latest model of family car. Special motoring clothing was also advertised in these magazines. An article in the second issue of the *The Car* of 1902 discusses the range of motoring overcoats available and who might be seen wearing what. Lilly Langtry is photographed in a sable coat from Redfern's, but the adventurous motorist would be encouraged to go for something more functional, perhaps from Dunhill's 'motorities'.

The magazines also highlight the hazards of motoring. Edwardian roads were still made up of compacted stone or gravel and in dry weather clouds of dust would be thrown up by the cars, choking and blinding the motorist before covering him with a fine white layer from head to foot. Whilst a light rain shower would provide perfect road conditions, anything more substantial would convert the fine dust into a thick creamy slime on which the intrepid motor-ist could easily be caught in a lethal skid. With no protective windscreen or waterproof hood most cars were put away for the winter months.

Articles on how best to respond to these conditions, together with the latest medical opinion on the potential damage that driving could do to the eyes and to the complexion, informed the motorist of the sorts of precautions that he or she might take. Fur-lined goggles with cotton or leather ankle-length dust coats were recommended for men, and ladies were encouraged to cover their delicate skin with special creams before donning Mica face masks which concealed all but the eyes. Later, more elegant veils were introduced for ladies; tied under the chin, they could also hold in place the fashionable wide-brimmed hats. The protective fur-lined sac coat seems to have been considered indispensable to the serious lady motorist in the colder months.

Edwardian ladies were clearly by no means confined to the passenger seat. In fact the lady driver appears to have been quite commonplace from the 1890s onward. At first they took on the relatively clean and odour-free electric cars of the end of the nineteenth century, but a *Punch* cartoon of 1903 shows the unaccompanied lady driver as very much the norm. By the end of the Edwardian period 'Stepney' were advertising their spare wheels being changed by lady motorists and Austro Daimler seemed to see their latest model of 1914 as the essential get-away car for every independent young woman of means.

Below: Cover of The Car, 1902, depicting King Edward VII, a great supporter of motoring.

Below: 'The Stepney Fixer' spare wheel was advertised as being easy and clean enough for a woman to change. Women motorists were already the norm by the turn of the century.

Above left and right: Special clothing was recommended to protect the motorist's eyes and face and large dust coats covered almost everything else. It didn't really matter what early motorists looked like in a Mica face mask or a pair of fur-lined goggles since they were disguised beyond recognition.

AustroDaimler

A LITTLE BETTER THAN SEEMS NECESSARY

16-25 h.p. "Alpine" Two-seater de luxe ready for immediate delivery. Duplicates in family colours, or to choice in three weeks. Complete specification and all details by return of post.

AUSTRIAN-DAIMLER MOTOR CO., Ltd., 112 Great Portland Street, London, W.

Telephone : 238 & 239 Gerrard.

Above: By 1914 glass windshields and removable car hoods were allowing the motorist to dress less cautiously and the new streamlined cars brought a fresh glamour to motoring.

Motoring remained the province of the wealthy in Edwardian London, although from 1905 serious attempts were being made to introduce a viable means of motorised public transport and by 1908 motor bus rides into the country were being offered at 8d per head. Speed limits had been raised to twenty miles per hour in 1903. Five years later the Model T Ford, a light, simple and sturdy car capable of being mass produced at a low price, first went into production in America. It was to become the universal family car. In 1909 twelve thousand motor cars were manufactured in Britain alone, the majority of which were being run on pneumatic tyres. It was this incentive which persuaded Michelin to expand into Britain.

Michelin bicycle tyres had been imported into England as early as 1891, but patents owned by Dunlop effectively prevented all other manufacturers from selling their tyres in Britain, except under licence, until the autumn of 1904. In April of that year Michelin took a small office in Tavistock Place, South Kensington, in anticipation of the expiry of the patents. Marc Wolff came over from France to be Company Secretary, bringing three other French employees with him. Fourteen additional staff were recruited locally. On 7 June 1905 the Michelin Tyre Company Limited was incorporated with André Michelin as Chairman. By the following year the staff had increased to forty-five. New premises were found and the company moved to Sussex Place, but it was evident that a much larger, more ambitious headquarters would be required and the search began for a site.

It would seem that the Michelin brothers had decided from the outset that they wanted to design a new building rather than continue to expand the essentially retail properties that they had rented in Sussex Place. They wanted a site that would be prominent, prestigious and easily accessible both to customers and to the fleet of vans delivering huge quantities of tyres. A number of different areas were looked at, including sites in Broad Street, Shaftesbury Avenue, Vauxhall Bridge Road and Alexander Square; the site bounded by the Fulham Road, Sloane Avenue, Lucan Place and Leader Street on which Michelin House was built was not offered to the company until June 1909.

The first known plans for a London office, for a two storey building on a site on the Vauxhall Bridge Road, are dated as early as 1906. The plans were drawn up by a 'B9', an identification for personnel from the building division at Clermont-Ferrand, with elevations by a 'B5'. In fact 'B9' is known to have been a M. François Espinasse, the designer responsible for the Michelin Building as it was finally built on the Fulham Road; 'B5' was a M. Delvert. We do not know to what extent Delvert and Espinasse worked together on the ideas for the design, but the elevation for Vauxhall Bridge Road of 23 February 1907 already shows a version of the 'Nunc est Bibendum' stained glass window and a similar style of lettering to that implemented three years later on the Fulham Road building. The Vauxhall Bridge Road drawings are tighter and more ornate than the later proposals for a head office. The ground floor windows are marked with 'enamelled crockery lettering' to describe the various Michelin products. There is also a curious reference on one of the drawings to 'Flash Lightning'; it seems more than likely that if neon had been invented by 1909 Espinasse and the Michelin brothers would have found a way of working it into the building.

The plans were never submitted for planning permission. Almost before they were fully worked out the company's attention was turned to a new site in Alexander Square facing the Fulham Road. Espinasse drew up two alternative schemes for the redevelopment of this site in November 1907, but the project was abandoned. Finally, in June 1909, the site in the Fulham Road was offered to Michelin.

The main attractions of the space were its convenience for prospective customers living in the Chelsea area and, more important, its location on one of the main exits from the city by car. This made it ideal both as a headquarters for a tyre distribution centre for the whole of Britain and as a centre where the customer could have his tyres checked, changed or repaired, plot his route or replenish his supply of petrol.

The site was part of a much larger area owned by the Cadogan & Hans Place Estate Ltd., and its sale was integrated into an overall plan to improve what was then a fairly run down area. The original building lines were set well back, effectively doubling the width of Sloane Avenue, and the lines of Little Keppel Street, which originally ran alongside and cut across the site,

Above: In 1908 a car was far beyond the means of most families. But a trip to Merstham by motor bus at 8d per head was a very attractive alternative for a Sunday treat.

Below: These 1907 elevations for a site in Vauxhall Bridge Road already incorporate ceramic lettering, small tyre cupolas, tyre and wheel motifs on pillars, and, most significantly, the Michelin man stained glass window. Although very attractive, both of these designs by Delbert show a stylistic tightness and conformity that was thrown to the wind in the final design for the Fulham Road building.

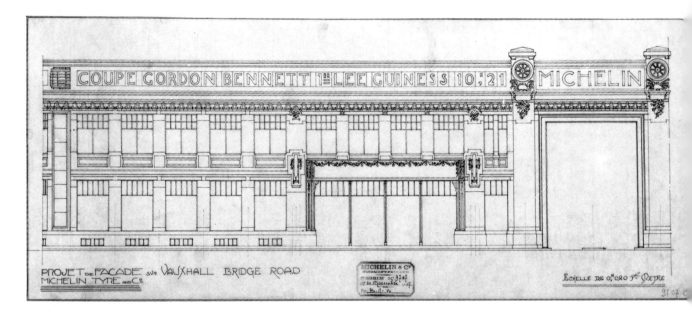

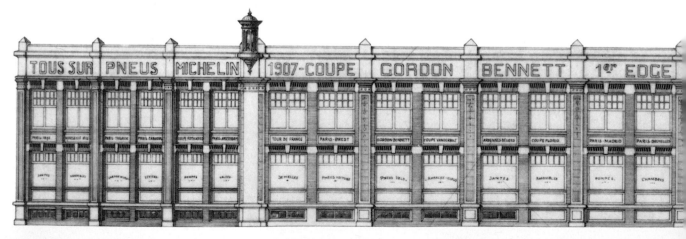

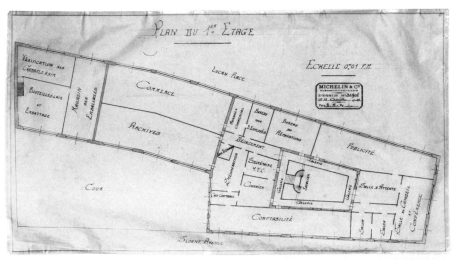

were altered to create the much wider Lucan Place. The basement plans show spaces for planting trees on the Sloane Avenue side and even today the basement walls are cut away to allow for these. Nevertheless, the new site was surrounded by small retail spaces, with the Admiral Keppel pub on the Sloane Avenue corner and a chimney cleaning establishment and wardrobe dealer at the rear.

The first plans for the Fulham Road site were drawn up by Delbert, or 'B5', in Clermont-Ferrand and are dated 29 August 1909. There are two alternative schemes, interesting today only as foils to the design that was actually carried out. Both of them show unimaginative layouts with the wedge-shaped site compartmentalised into quite small, geometrically shaped rooms. There are none of the sweeping curves and generously proportioned rooms of the

later design, nor is there any evidence of the logical progression of functions moving from storage at the rear through to the tyre fitting bay and rooms where the customer might be made comfortable at the front of the building. Both schemes envisage only a ground floor and first floor and far less of the site is initially developed, with a larger area reserved for future extensions.

The plans were never presented for planning permission. Nor were they accompanied by any elevations and, unlike their successors, they are worded entirely in French. Evidently they were never intended to be taken any further, and it seems that 'B5' was taken off the British headquarters after these early explorations because almost all of the later drawings are marked 'B9', which was François Espinasse's identification.

Below: The earliest plans for the Fulham Road building, by Delbert, were a far cry from the generous open plan offices designed by Espinasse a few months later. There are two alternative designs, both dated 29 August 1909. This first floor plan shows a traditionally grand central staircase surrounded by neatly squared off offices and corridors.

t is surprising that so little is known about the designer of the Michelin Building, considering its architectural importance. François Espinasse was not a qualified architect. The French Order of Architects in Paris have no record of him and the only other building that he is known to have designed is Michelin's Paris headquarters at 97 boulevard Péreire. Apart from three large tiled panels showing the Michelin man on the front façade, the Paris building is quite unremarkable. The Fulham Road building represents a radical departure from contemporary architecture that was never to be repeated.

Espinasse was born in Vic le Conte on 1 August 1880 and he joined the Service des Bâtiments, or Building Division, of Michelin's Clermont-Ferrand factory on 12 February 1906, just a year before the Vauxhall Bridge Road drawings. He lived with his wife and four children at rue Vernemouze, Quartier Rabanesse, Clermont-Ferrand. In 1908 he worked for a time in Paris, presumably overseeing the construction of the headquarters there, and in 1911 he is known to have been working in London, although we do not know the exact date of his arrival. He continued to work for Michelin until his early death at the age of forty-four on 2 May 1925; he received no obituary in either the French architectural press or the local Clermont newspaper *La Montagne*.

It is disappointing that so extraordinary a building should be an isolated achievement in an otherwise uneventful career. But in a sense it is not especially surprising. The Michelin Building is not the expression of one man's creativity: it is the physical realisation of the ideals and aspirations of a company. André and Edouard Michelin, the two driving forces behind that company, both had artistic backgrounds. André trained as an architect at the Ecole des Beaux Arts from 1877 and Edouard trained there as a painter. They were men of exceptional vision, ambition and commitment, renowned for their involvement in every aspect of the company, and it is very likely that they would have had a considerable influence on the design of their new London head office.

Espinasse's first sketch of the Fulham Road building dates from 29 October 1909. A radical departure from all of his previous drawings, this sketch, although outrageously exaggerated, embodies the spirit of the building. Its main characteristics – the triple entrance, corner turrets, tyre cupolas, vertical 'Michelin' lettering, shaped gable and main decorated central window – are all there in essence. The fact that the drawing bears more resemblance to a child's imaginative fantasy than to a serious architectural proposal is perhaps intrinsic to a vision of this kind. The sketch, for obvious reasons, was not presented to the planning authorities. Nor were the three finished façade drawings which followed it nearly five weeks later. They were part of eleven plans and elevations, all dated 1 December 1909.

These charming drawings began to rationalise the ideas of the first sketch. In the front elevation, the 'Michelin' panels have moved across to precariously protruding corner turrets and the central window has been split into three zones: a semi-circular 'Nunc

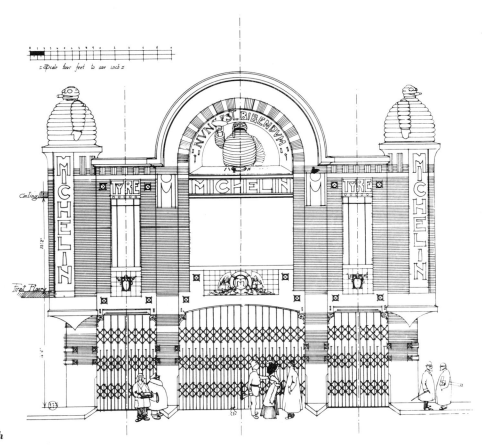

Left: Espinasse's first sketch for the building, dated 29 October 1909, shows an extraordinary exuberance, but the key features of the final design are already established.
Above right: This earliest elevation on Fulham Road, of 1 December 1909, has an almost Art Deco boldness.

est Bibendum' section, a narrow horizontal 'Michelin' band and a lower section left plain. Tall windows to either side have appeared and, as in the final design, these have decorative panels above and below (although these were to change) and the three entrances are fitted with ornate wrought iron gates. An interesting selection of people are drawn standing in front of these. Here Espinasse is surely having some fun. It has been suggested that the three groups represent a match-seller and a cabbie; a little dog peering through the gates next to a police constable, who is arresting a lady of the night, and two gentlemen in conversation, who just might be André Michelin (with pronounced beard) and Espinasse himself.

The remaining ten drawings showed plans and cross sections of the three floors as they were actually to be built, and slightly amended side elevations. They were submitted to the Superintending Architect's Department of London County Council on 15 January 1910. Clearly, Espinasse must have seen that the Fulham Road elevation, with its fat cigar-smoking Michelin men sitting jauntily on the turrets, was too eccentric: a later alternative of 16 December 1909 was submitted instead.

This revised design shows a surprising stylistic shift so that it is quite incompatible with its accompanying Lucan Place and Sloane Avenue elevations. The central Bibendum stained glass window remains relatively unchanged. But the bold 'Michelin' lettering below has been replaced by an ornate Art Nouveau style 'Michelin Tyre

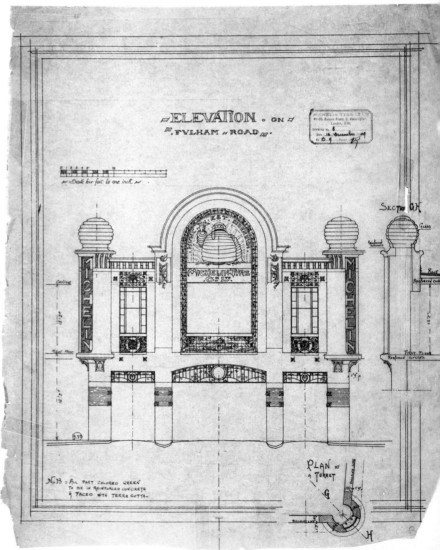

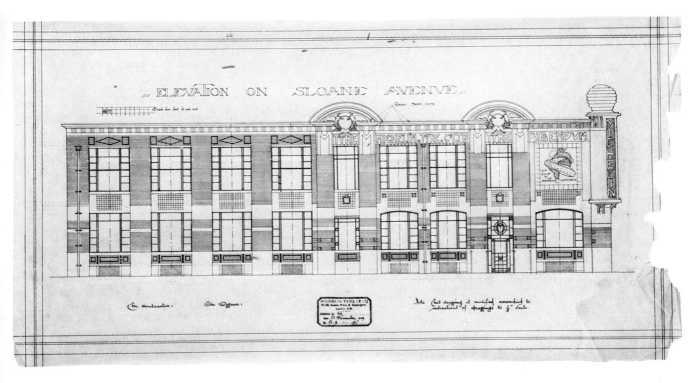

Above: Elevation on Sloane Avenue, 1 December 1909.

Left: Just over two weeks after the first elevation this drawing of 16 December 1909 replaced the angular geometric lines with decorative Art Nouveau motifs. Sadly the Michelin men cupolas have lost their arms, heads, legs and cigars to become almost spherical forms made up of tyres.

Co. Ltd.', and the winged tyre motif at the base (which was adopted from an early Michelin poster) has been transposed with a picture of a racing car, possibly in tiles, framed, like the later tiles, by Art Nouveau foliage. The entire window area is surrounded by intertwining tendrils which reappear, rather less convincingly, from behind the elongated 'M' on the pillars to either side. The two smaller front windows now show tyres, for the first time embedded in foliage, and the bold 'Tyre' lettering of the previous drawing has been replaced by a diamond shaped 'MTC' monogram. The angular wrought iron gates have been removed and delicately curving lintels incorporating the rounded 'M' letter sit ornamentally above the three main entrances. Some suggestion of the 'Marmo' bands on the tower shaft becomes evident and, perhaps most significantly from the planning point of view, the dangerous original overhang of the turrets is substantially reduced. Sadly the enormous Michelin men cupolas have lost their arms, heads and cigars to become more ambiguous spherical objects. As the first Lucan Place and Sloane Avenue elevations had already had those features erased, perhaps they had never been seriously envisaged in their more human form.

The elevations for Sloane Avenue and Lucan Place are very close structurally to the final version, but they have a neatness and elongated elegance that was replaced by a much bolder statement in the design that was actually built. The winged tyre motifs in the shaped pediments are much more delicate and the 'MTC' capitals are

here represented by a simple 'M'; the frieze-like lettering is already in place in a highly stylised form, but the interlocking tyre motifs between the ground floor and first floor windows are represented by a simple crest and grid pattern; the stained glass window of Bibendum showing the sole of his boot is already devised on the Sloane Avenue elevation, although it is smaller with a simple grid pattern beneath. But on the Lucan Place side the stained glass area is left as a completely plain grid. Presumably at this stage it was planned as an ordinary window. There is no evidence to suggest otherwise.

All three elevations have an ornate delicacy that was entirely lacking in both the original sketch and the final design, which was much stronger, more idiosyncratic, and provided

the appropriate vehicle for the proclamation that the Michelin brothers had envisaged: the Michelin Tyre Company had arrived in Britain. It is almost as though, having invented the component parts that would make up his building, Espinasse was trying in these drawings of early December to integrate them into an existing and acceptable architectural style. These December plans, which show a painstaking attention to detail quite at odds with the brash razzmatazz of the elevations, were rejected by the LCC on 15 January 1910. They were resubmitted with only minor alterations and with the new set of elevations on 11 October 1910 and two weeks later they were passed by W. E. Riley, the Superintending Architect. The design of the new British Michelin headquarters was agreed and ready to implement.

Left: The final designs for the building, dated 4 April 1910: elevation on Fulham Road, (opposite above) elevation of Lucan Place, (opposite below) elevation on Sloane Avenue.

Below: The Touring Office. Contemporary advertisements suggested '... why not smoke a cigarette over the latest illustrated papers, or write a letter or two?' Pens, ink, paper and stamps were supplied.

The design of the Michelin Building to make a strong visual impact is often commented upon. But the building's ability to fulfil a considerable range of functions, through careful planning, is often overlooked. It had to accommodate the growing managerial and clerical staff responsible for running the British division of Michelin, to provide space for the storage and distribution of tyres for the whole of Britain and, finally, to provide a retail outlet where customers could come and purchase tyres and, if necessary, have them fitted. This last retailing function gave rise to a whole host of associated services including a garage where customers could purchase petrol, a Touring Office and a tyre fitting bay, as well as a salesroom.

The Motor magazine of 24 January 1911 devoted a full illustrated page to the opening of the building.

> As one approaches the iron-framed doors, they quietly and without external aid open to give one entrance, a feature which is distinctly novel and also possesses the not always correlative attribute of utility. Once inside, one finds one-self in a spacious hall, all along the upper end of which runs a substantial counter at which one may make one's inquiries and obtain instanter [sic] any size of cycle or motor tyre or, for that matter, any of the numerous Michelin accessories. On the left of this hall is a room set aside solely for the convenience and utility of customers ... At the

> back of the aforementioned counter are sliding doors which communicate with the day stockrooms, and in the course of our visit we saw several people inquire for tubes, tyres, etc., which were forthcoming in the space of about a minute and a half. This stockroom, as its name indicates, is arranged with sufficient quantities of all the different tyres, etc., to supply any ordinary demands that may be made upon it in the course of a day without the slightest waiting, being replenished from the main stores afterwards. To the rear and left of the entrance-hall is the repair department, with the staff of experts for repairing – reporting upon the probable efficacy of instituting repairs – or for actually doing the work as the case may be. Passing on one comes to the main stores, and the arrival and departure platforms for the different vans, whether the company's own despatching vans or the various carrier vans that may be delivering goods. Conveniently situated hereabouts is a garage, where the vans, etc., are accommodated.

The basement, which stocked some 25,000 tyre covers and 30,000 tubes, extends under the pavement by 5'7" on the Lucan Place side and by 7'3" under Sloane Avenue, in order to make the fullest use of the available storage space. A 10 cwt Pickerings goods lift linked the storage area with the tyre packing room on the ground floor.

The concept of office accommodation was still very much in its infancy in 1909 and the first floor Michelin offices, which had to be reached by stairs, were straightforward and unassuming. Their concrete floors were left uncovered, but they made full use of the structural advantages of concrete by retaining an open plan, following the example set by Frank Lloyd Wright's Larkin building of 1904. The *Motor* report goes on to describe them as 'Commodious, well-lit, and well-aired and everything throughout the premises tells its own tale of efficiency.'

This efficiency is carried through in an imaginative attention to detail throughout the building. Almost a hundred drawings make up the specifications for the building, excluding the structural drawings. On driving through the main gate into the tyre fitting bay the customer would park his car on a 6 ton weighbridge so that mechanics below might work out the exact tyre pressure required. If the motorist had time on his hands whilst his new tyres were being fitted he might take advantage of the facilities of the Touring Office, where contemporary advertisements suggested:

> ...one may write or consult the maps and touring guides, etc. in quiet and comfort. On the wall are arranged a series of excellent roll-up maps dealing not only with the United Kingdom, but also with France, Italy, Switzerland, etc., so that by merely pulling down the desired map one has an excellent work of reference as regards roads, itineraries, etc.

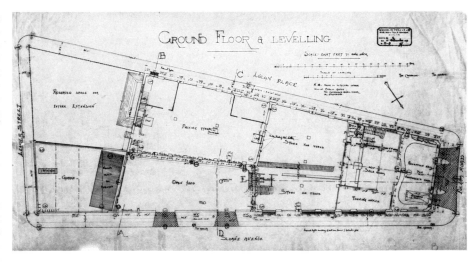

The Touring Office exemplified Michelin's interest in every aspect of motoring. Throughout the building one department led directly on to its appropriate neighbour, so that space was not wasted unnecessarily in corridors, and the entire ground floor sloped slightly from the store room at the rear through to the salesroom at the front so that tyres could more easily be rolled through.

From the grandeur of automatic doors through to the detailing of an early telephone kiosk, the design of the building anticipated every requirement that might be made of it. For all its razzle-dazzle on the outside, the design of the interior of the Michelin Building must be recognised as a model combination of functionalism, affluence and stylish modernity.

Above: The ground floor plan of the building, dated 1 December 1909, shows the logical progression of rooms from one function to the next, retaining a generous sense of space.

Below: This photograph of a
Michelin promotion,
probably taken in October
1911 to coincide with the
motor show at Olympia,
reveals a poster or advertising
screen in the glass box area
below the central window.
Left and below right: The front
and the Sloane Avenue side of
the building shortly after it
opened. The two ceramic
royal crests which were to be
situated below the front windows were not yet in place; the
photographs were neatly
blanked out to hide the raw
brick where they were to go.

When the Michelin Building first opened in January 1911 it must have stunned local residents and passers-by with its audacious irreverence. The new London offices were to be a permanent expression of Michelin's aggressive, imaginative, witty and direct advertising campaign, shouting the name at every passing driver. The building's use of colour and surface texture, bold lettering and impudent incorporation of tyre motifs and advertising imagery combine to make it a unique London landmark even today.

Three huge stained glass windows showing Bibendum, the Michelin man, dominated the front portion of the building. If this fat man made up of tyres was thought to be an unsuitable subject for the adornment of a building, then the depiction of some of his exploits must have been seen as highly undesirable. He is shown riding a bicycle, cigar characteristically in one hand, the other in his pocket; posing as a kicking boxer showing the studded sole of a boot; on the front of the building raising a champagne glass of sharp objects likely to puncture a tyre.

Burmantofts' 'Marmo' tiles, a relatively new and untested material, were used to clad the entire front façade of the building and portions of the adjacent walls in white, blue, yellow and green, making a great impact on the building press of the time. *The Building News* of 27 January 1911 reports that :

> One's interest is arrested by the exclusive and beautiful style of Burmantofts' 'Marmo' facing, in

several colours, with enriched emblematic and heraldic patterns supplied by the Leeds Fireclay Company Ltd.

And the *Architects' and Builders' Journal* of 8 February writes that:

> ...the facing has been executed in Burmantofts' 'Marmo' in several colours ... a pleasing surface which successfully resists the action of weather and, what is of special importance, can be periodically cleaned of all soot and dirt.

Coloured buildings were still very unusual in 1911 and the brilliant white face, off-set with blue rusticated pedestals, would have stood out sharply against its surroundings. Blue-green vertical ribbons are inset into the central columns, which flank the main entrance to the building, and the same colour is used in wide horizontal bands over the three entrances and the two ground floor side windows to give a semblance of architectural unity. But at every conceivable opportunity traditional decorative motifs have been whipped out. In their place are the most extraordinary adornments skilfully incorporating an imaginative assortment of tyre related images.

If the stained glass windows were not self-explanatory, then the blue ceramic 'Bibendum' directly above them, continuing 'Michelin Tyre Co. Ltd.' down each side of the building, made sure that the message got across. Classical capitals heading the two central columns on the front façade and the four columns down either side

were replaced by a superbly worked 'MTC' monogram raised in white against blue. But this lettering is positively traditional by comparison with the vertical panels on each of the tower shafts where 'Michelin' is spelt out in the company colours of yellow on dark blue glass. At night time these panels, topped by enormous yellow glass cupolas made up of a series of tyres, were illuminated. According to local residents the central stained glass window was also lit up by mercury vapour lamps, giving a ghostly blue-grey light, and one of the drawings clearly shows a light bulb behind the plain window below.

This window remains something of a mystery. In a number of 1911 photographs it clearly contains an image of Bibendum holding up an axle, with the words 'Twin Tyre. Heavy Cars.' This is consistent with Michelin advertising of the time. Espinasse's drawings show a box form with a removable lid where advertising screens or banners could be dropped in. It would seem inconsistent to leave the most prominent area of so decorated a building completely plain and yet only the one image is known to have been used. There are no known photographs of the building between 1912 and the end of the Second World War, but later photographs show an empty box.

Ceramic plaques decorate the building with a variety of three-dimensional tyre images. Set within the two curved pedestals on either side of the building, a yellow and white wheel is shown solidly set into pale green foliage with red berries. The same greenery appears in the panels below, intertwined between three interlocking wheels with a central rounded 'M'. In fact, is not random greenery at all but a clearly identifiable species of rubber plant! More wheels emerge from their leaves and berries on the front façade of the building over the two side windows. Above the tower shafts on either side of the shaped gable enormous yellow studded tyres stand up against the sky. The ceramic plaques, like the faiencing, were produced by the Leeds Fireclay Company, who had their own specialist team of artists and would have prepared their own working drawings from Espinasse's rough sketches. The plaque would first have been cast in plaster of Paris moulds and then fired.

The Michelin Building is almost over-endowed with decorative features embracing a variety of styles and preoccupations but perhaps the most notable decoration at close quarters are the thirty-four tiled pictures around the outside and leading into the entrance hall of the building. Surprisingly the tiles were almost completely ignored by the contemporary architectural and motoring press. Set well above eye level, the tiles were probably intended to be viewed from the high Edwardian cars These pictures tell the story of the importance of Michelin tyres to the history of motoring, from Charles Terront in the 1891 Paris to Brest race through to King Edward VII in a chauffeur-driven Sedanca de Ville. Most of the tiles were replicas of a set used in the Paris headquarters, the only physical link between the two buildings. They represent the most subtle of advertising images incorporated into the building.

BIBENDUM

Above: The ceramic lettering and the three-dimensional faience blocks under the eaves of the roof were all in good condition and when they were cleaned their original colours were brilliantly reinstated.

Above: The Michelin Building just before it changed hands in 1985.

Right: O'Galop's first image of Bibendum, the Michelin man. He was to form the basis not only for the Fulham Road stained glass window but also Michelin's image all over the world.

Below: 'The Most Sumptuous Clubhouse in the World', the RAC building in Pall Mall, opened a few months after the Michelin building.

The Michelin Building could have been designed to embody the opulence and glamour of early motoring. The RAC building, 'The Most Sumptuous Clubhouse in the World', opened just a few months after it in Pall Mall with a grand Portland stone façade and a wonderfully mosaiced Turkish bath and swimming pool. On a more modest scale, the Lancia showroom of the same date at 26 Albemarle Street, Piccadilly, gives a good example of the sleek and stylish motoring discretion apparently meeting all of the requirements set out in *The Car* magazine of January 1911:

> *A showroom for automobiles should convey a sense of luxury in conformity with the inherent and comparative expensiveness of the article itself. This luxury should, however, be of a solid kind, simple in taste, but good — a high class background, against which the polished chassis, the beautifully finished landaulette, will stand out, and yet be enhanced in appearance by the surroundings, and which all the same will show off the modest open car that is in keeping with, but equally improved by, its setting. Let there be as much frontage as possible to the street, or at any rate an appearance of spaciousness when inside, and, if the place lacks room somewhat, be content with a small array of cars, which can easily be inspected by a lady without squeezing past other vehicles, and possibly greasing or soiling her clothes.'*

The Michelin Building was certainly spacious and in its own way luxurious. But simple in taste and a high class background, Michelin House was much more the architectural expression of an extremely lively and innovative advertising campaign than a monument to the solidity and expansiveness of its company. Competition for the British tyre market was hot and Michelin were undercutting their competitors at the time of the opening of the building.

Few companies could boast a more imaginative approach to publicity. Stunts in France included a cycle race from Paris to Clermont-Ferrand booby trapped with patches of nails to exemplify the ease of repairing detachable pneumatics. In Paris staff were planted *en masse* on an autobus so that they could dismount all at once and to the delight of a tipped-off press, take up poses on a passing pig truck, which, of course, used Michelin pneumatics. But perhaps the most important invention in the Michelin campaign was the creation of Bibendum, the Michelin man.

Before the Bibendum images Michelin posters were similar in style and content to a multitude of other French posters of the last decade of the nineteenth century. Scantily clad ladies waft through the air on winged tyres whilst deflated and dejected competitors are left watching miserably on the sidelines. It was not until 1898 that the image of the pneumatic-bodied, cigar smoking and decidedly amusing figure of Bibendum swept the classical muses aside to become Michelin's international logo.

Michelin

Left: This poster marks a transition in Michelin's advertising from Art Nouveau muses to bold Bibendum statements.
Above: 'The Wheel of Fortune', an early Michelin poster based on a drawing by Edouard Michelin.

Above: The new stained glass window on the front of the building, replacing the lost original, is based on the first O'Galop poster.

Above right: 'Now is the time to drink.' Bibendum raises a champagne glass of sharp objects, demonstrating the repairability of Michelin pneumatics.
Near right: One of the advertising images on which the Lucan Place stained glass window was based; Bibendum the intrepid cyclist speeds along, whilst distributing his midriff bulges to anyone in need of a spare tyre.
Far right: 'Rien à faire Messieurs, c'est une Semelle Michelin!'

Below: Stained glass window on the Sloane Avenue side based on, bottom, a poster of Bib as a kicking boxer. The sole of his boot is steel — studded like a non-skid 'Semelle' tyre.

Legend has it that the first idea for Bibendum came to André and Edouard Michelin as they looked at a stand of their tyres, piled up in an assortment of sizes at a trade show. Edouard is reputed to have said, 'If it had arms it would look like a man.' Shortly afterwards the poster artist O'Galop visited the brothers with his portfolio, hoping for a commission. He had with him a cartoon for a German beer manufacturer showing a large Bavarian raising his beer mug; the words read 'Nunc est Bibendum' (Now is the time to drink) from one of Horace's *Odes*. The brothers asked O'Galop if he could repeat the figure, but make him look as though he were made up of tyres. In the first Bibendum poster the beer mug was replaced by a champagne glass filled with sharp obstacles and the slogan 'Nunc est Bibendum' is extended to include 'Le Pneu Michelin boit l'obstacle.' Bibendum stuck as the name for the Michelin man when, at the 1898 Paris-Amsterdam race held a few months after the poster came out, one of the drivers called out after André Michelin 'Look, there is Bibendum.' The brothers accepted the name as summing up both the company and their new cartoon character.

Some of the earliest Bibendum posters have a painterly, almost eerie quality. One, by A. Renault, advertising a cycle tyre, sets the more traditional figure of a frothily dressed lady into the very human hand of a rather ghostly Bibendum; we are reminded of the less convincing Bibendum figure on the Vauxhall Bridge Road elevation. But the posters signed by O'Galop have the directness and humour of the earliest examples

and it is these images that are used to decorate the Michelin Building. The images were taken straight from publicity campaigns and transposed into permanent building materials to form a unique blend of advertising and architecture.

The huge arch-shaped, stained glass window on the front of the building is an adaptation of the first O'Galop poster. There are two slightly different versions of the poster and the window relates most closely to the later one. Bibendum is shown cuff-linked and monocled, raising his glass of sharp objects, with the slogan 'Nunc est Bibendum' filling the arch above his head. He sits at a table, perhaps in expectation of Michelin's restaurant guides and in front of him are set out all the tools and materials necessary for repairing a Michelin tyre. To his extreme right are a selection of tyre levers, including an elbow lever and a spur lever for removing tyres. Next to these is a compressed air bottle, in front of which sits a small box spanner. On a plate next to the air bottle there is an assortment of patches and to the right of these is a tin of mastic for plugging holes in the outer corners (Michelin made their own mastic). To the right of this tin is a bolt valve hood and, just in front of Bibendum's hand, there is a fork lever. A second and simplified version of the same image is repeated in mosaic on the entrance hall floor; again the detailing extends right down to a gold ring on the little finger of Bibendum's left hand.

The stained glass window on the Lucan Place side, showing Bibendum riding a bicycle, one hand tucked confidently into

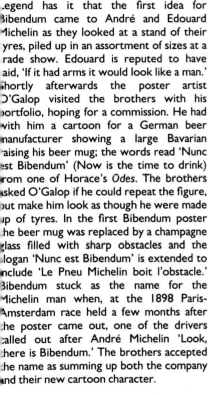

Above: The Michelin stand at the Olympia motor show, 1910. Bibendum shows off his 'Semelle' waist line and knees. Even his shoes are studded.

his pocket and the other wafting a cigar, again taken from a publicity poster, this time for 'Michelin Cycle Tyre'. But perhaps the most outrageous of the three stained glass window images is the one on the Sloane Avenue side. Again the source is an O'Galop poster, this time advertising the 'Semelle' tyre.

First produced in June 1905, the 'Semelle' tyre was Michelin's answer to 'the dreaded side slip'. Quite ordinary cars were now capable of speeds of up to sixty miles per hour and for inexperienced drivers in heavy vehicles with relatively high centres of gravity the danger of skidding on unmade-up roads was very real indeed.

The 'Semelle' tyre was promoted as:

> Non-skid and largely puncture proof because of its special steel rivet lining permanently fixed to the cover with a leather band vulca-nised at the same time as the cover to prevent detachment.

The steel studs must have made a terrific noise as they were driven along the road, but the 'Semelle' was obviously a good seller and it appears in a number of places on the Michelin Building.

The bright yellow tyres on either side of the shaped gable are obviously 'Semelle' and the image for the stained glass window was first used in ceramic tiles on the Paris headquarters. It is taken directly from the O'Galop poster where the artist has drawn Bib as a boxer complete with leopard skin shorts. French boxers at the turn of the century were allowed to box with their feet and hands; here Bib is shown packing a punch with an unfair advantage.

The unique boldness of O'Galop's work is well illustrated by two other posters for the 'Semelle' of around the same date. The first is a simple information sheet for the British market, and the second is a French poster by Flink. The principle of the 'Semelle' tyre is the same as that used on shoe soles of the time, which were also studded, and Flink has chosen to show a well-dressed lady driving rather snootily past two ageing cobblers with the slogan 'Rien à faire, Messieurs, c'est une Semelle Michelin!' The image is attractively drawn and humorously conceived, but it lacks the punch of the O'Galop poster.

The 'Semelle' was still being promoted with great Michelin style at the Motor Show at Olympia in November 1910. The publicity for the Michelin stand at this show coincided with Michelin's change of address publicity and the two campaigns were cleverly integrated. It was perhaps particularly appropriate that these inspired and sensitively drawn advertisements, which express so succinctly the wit, vivacity, and imagination of the Michelin Company, should have been used to herald the opening of its most sensational piece of publicity: an advertisement realised in architectural proportions. And so the audacity of incorporating advertisements into the fabric of architecture is reflected back in advertisements with carefully rendered line drawings of the building integrated in their design.

Left: 'The Rail Vanquished by Michelin Tyres'. Ernest Montaut's 1904 poster for Michelin.

Opposite above: The 1903 Paris-Madrid was the last of the great capital to capital races. Between 300 and 400 people were killed due to inadequate spectator control and the event became known as 'The Race of Death'.

Opposite below: As well as races the tiles also show the great long distance challenges like Hemery's 438 mile drive from St. Petersburg to Moscow.

The thirty-four tiled pictures, which decorate the brick columns around the outside of the building just above eye level and continue round into the tyre fitting bay and reception area, represent a more subtle form of advertising. Michelin's involvement in the history of early racing, starting with the first cycle race with Charles Terront in 1891, was an important element in their marketing policy and the tiles depict the racing successes of cars with Michelin tyres. Most of them are replicas of a set originally made for the Paris headquarters. Gilardoni Fils et Cie of 38 rue du Paradis, Paris, went out of business shortly after making this second set and it is likely that so complicated a commission of one-off tiles tipped the balance towards their bankruptcy. Standards in ceramics and glassware in Paris at the turn of the century were exceptionally high and Gilardoni's previous panels although of a more traditional nature incorporating landscape and floral designs are consistently fine. This second set of Michelin panels, however, are very mixed in quality, ranging from the finest work to positively bad draughtsmanship, and it has been suggested that only a company past caring about its reputation would have allowed some of the pictures to go through. Whilst some of the panels were clearly made by Gilardoni himself, in others artists who would normally be used only for filling in work seem to have been allowed to trace, copy and even draw in the details. The drawing is laboured and one of the tiles is actually drawn back to front, as though it has been traced from the Paris original and not corrected. Nevertheless, the tiles represent a stunning feature.

The images for the tiles are taken from a set of drawings by Ernest Montaut. Montaut, a poster artist who specialised in racing images, often invented the techniques that we now accept as standard methods of suggesting speed and excitement. In 1904 he designed a poster for Michelin showing 'The Rail Vanquished by Michelin Tyres'. The commission to design a set of tile panels must have been one of the last that he completed because he died in 1909 at the age of thirty-one. The fact that later scenes from 1909 and 1910 races are included would suggest that these were manufactured in 1910 from drawings made either by Ernest Montaut's wife or by one of the other artists employed by his firm, which was still in existence, listed as Montaut et Cie, in 1914.

Other tiles like 'Gabriel sur Mors' in the Paris-Madrid race of 1903 tell the story of early racing. This race, now known as 'The Race of Death', was the last of the great capital to capital courses and marked the end of an era in motor racing. Set to take place in three stages – from Versailles to Bordeaux, from Pessac to Vittoria and from Vittoria to Madrid, the race was organised to start on a Sunday to allow the maximum number of spectators. There were 275 competitors, who set off at intervals of just one minute, and, with practically no spectator control, the excited crowd parted just enough to let each car hurtle through before closing up again. Accidents began to occur as one car crashed into another. Marcel Renault, pictured on a Michelin tile as the winner of the previous year's Paris-Vienne, was one of the first fatalities and by the end of the day between 300 and 400 drivers and spectators had been killed or injured. Governments intervened and the race was called off at Bordeaux. Because there was no outright winner both Gabriel and Louis Renault are featured on the Michelin tiles, each driving on Michelin pneumatics.

Races became confined to specific courses, like the 'Circuit de Brescia', and long drives on the open roads were limited to individual feats such as Hemery's 438 mile journey in a Benz from St. Petersburg to Moscow in 1908 (which, incidentally, was clearly not drawn by Gilardoni himself). Hemery was killed by a flying splinter of glass later in the same year at the Grand-Prix in Dieppe, superbly represented here on the Michelin tiles by a portrait of the

PARIS-MADRID
1903

GABRIEL sur
MORS

St PETERSBOURG
MOSCOU 1908

HEMERY
sur BENZ

Above: The tiles had to be faithfully copied into ceramic by Gilardoni Fils et Cie from Ernest Montaut's original drawings. This one of Lautenschlager was probably made by Gilardoni himself. Right: The tile depicting Minoia in his Isotta Fraschini is an excellent example of Montaut's ability to capture the speed, excitement and thrilling concentration of early motor racing.

winner Lautenschlager in his Mercedes. Lautenschlager's co-driver had been injured in the Franco-Prussian war and it is a testament to Gilardoni's skill on the better panels that this facial deformity is faithfully and convincingly represented.

It is perhaps one of the wittier qualities of these tiles that as racing speeds increased over the years, so the stylised indications of speed on the panels are used to greater effect. The dashing vitality and brilliant colour of Minoia winning the 1907 Coupe Florio Brescia in an Isotta Fraschini is an example of motoring art at its best, giving every indication of the speed of the race Minoia finished minus a nearside front tyre!

Montaut's original drawings for the tiles show a sharp observation and thorough understanding of the mechanics of early motoring as well as conveying the danger, concentration, and excitement of these early races. The cars themselves are so carefully detailed that you can see quite clearly that an early Renault had shaft drive as opposed to chain drive like most of the others and that Théry's Richard Brassier had shock absorbers, giving him the edge in the 1904 Gordon Bennett race. The original blue and yellow chequered border around each of the drawings, however, has been translated into Art Nouveau oak leaves on both sets of tiles. The reasons for this are unclear and one can only suppose that they were financial. Art Nouveau foliage was very often used as a standard frame for motoring and mechanical advertisements; perhaps they seemed less incongruous in 1910.

Only three of the tiled panels do not show the racing successes of Michelin tyres. They depict the first horse-drawn cab on Michelin pneumatics, 'Latham's Machine fitted with Michelin Aeroplane Sheeting', and King Edward VII and the Prince of Wales in a Sedanca de Ville — on Michelin tyres. This last is the only panel that is not framed by the copper coloured intertwining branches, oak leaves, and acorns and it forms the centre piece in the entrance hall. Made up of smaller, more detailed tiles with a richer glaze, it is likely that this panel, which is based on a photograph in the Royal Archive, was made in England. It celebrates the royal warrant that was granted to Marc Wolff as managing director of the Michelin Tyre Co. Ltd., in February 1908. Unfortunately, Edward VII died in May 1910. However, the warrant was endorsed by the Earl of Granard on 14 October 1910, dating the tile towards the end of that year.

King Edward VII's death delayed the making of two Burmantofts ceramic royal arms to sit below each of the side front windows, so that a photograph taken early in 1911 shows these as spaces left in bare brick. The arms appear in a slightly later photograph, but at that time the royal warrant was given to an individual within a company. When that person, in this case Marc Wolff, died or left the company the warrant expired. Marc Wolff resigned in November 1918, but Michelin remained on the list of royal warrant holders until 1927. At some time after that date the ceramic panels were removed and the crest above the tiled picture was painted over thinly with a gilt 'M'.

COUPE FLORIO
BRESCIA 1907

MINOÏA sur
ISOTTA-FRASCHINI

Left: 'A Well Appointed
Salesroom.'

The Touring Office in the Michelin Building, an idea first used in the Paris headquarters, gives a good indication of the imagination, confidence and breadth of interest André and Edouard Michelin showed in everything to do with motoring. Here motorists could plan their routes and itineraries by consulting the Michelin guides and maps.

Even in 1911 touring by motor car must have been a bewildering experience: as late as 1909 there were no town signs to tell motorists the name of the place they were driving through. Signposting generally was very poor throughout Europe. Michelin designed name boards that could be suspended from a bracket over roads going into each of the towns in France and these were presented as gifts to the local authorities. They recommended careful driving,

but at the same time they formed yet another, albeit more dignified, element in the Michelin advertising campaign. Another far more impertinent move by the brothers in the cause of improving motoring conditions was to persuade the French President to sign a large and impressive register at their stand at a trade show in 1912. The President assumed that he had signed a visitors' book until he was informed by a wave of publicity that it had in fact been a petition addressed to one of his own ministers demanding that roads should be properly numbered and signed to assist motorists in keeping to their routes!

André Michelin had begun his career as a minor official in the Ministry of the Interior Map Department. This early introduction to cartography instilled in him a life-long passion for maps that was expressed in the first Michelin Guide of 1900. The foreword boasted that:

> *This book is born at the same time as the new century and it will last as long. Motoring has just begun. It will develop and tyres will develop alongside the car for tyres are essential if cars are to move. Every year we shall publish a new careful revised edition.*

Until the 1920s Michelin Red Guides of France were given free to motorists. As there were only 35,000 in the whole of France when the first Guide was produced it represented a very considerable commitment to an idea in terms of the work and money involved. This first Guide included 1,410 towns, listed alphabetically, and informed the motorist of the best places to sleep, buy petrol and find garage facilities. It established the Michelin reputation as an unbiased arbiter of standards and the easily identifiable symbols that have been maintained ever since.

From the outset the Guides were attractively laid out with full-page maps of major routes and towns. Bibendum appears in a multitude of guises throughout the Guides. He is shown writing a letter, signalling a train to leave on time, in the role of a judge admonishing a recalcitrant motorist, or proudly advising on tyre maintenance in full-page Michelin advertisements printed in black and red. Full-colour maps are featured at the back of the Guides, together with pink information pages detailing all the facts that the international tourist might require.

By the end of 1910 there were Michelin Guides to France, the Benelux, Switzerland, Spain and Portugal, and to Algeria and Tunisia (a reflection of the French colonial sphere). The first Michelin Guide to Britain and Ireland was published in 1911, the same year in which the new British offices reopened. In over 560 pages it listed nearly 1,500 towns, gave 154 town plans, 29 regional maps and 68 pages of expert advice on tyre maintenance. Its carefully researched and detailed information included steamship fares and times, speed calculations, local taxation and licensing, the nearest hospitals, post offices, railway stations and golf courses, and, last but not least, aspects of motoring law.

Michelin's Map and Guide Office began with one employee at the Paris headquarters in 1908. But by 1919, when the office reopened after its wartime closure, it was dealing with 3,000 requests for routes and by 1924 a hundred were employed to respond to the 150,000 requests that were received each year. In 1926 Michelin began to publish regional guides which to some extent incorporated the individual itineraries and these quickly became a great success, selling 214,000 copies between 1926 and 1932. The first Michelin Map to be published independently of the Guides was of France and was produced after several years of preparation in 1910. As with the Guides a range of Michelin Maps soon appeared and became a great public success. The consistently high quality and regular updating of both Guides and Maps have ensured their continued public demand and critical reputation.

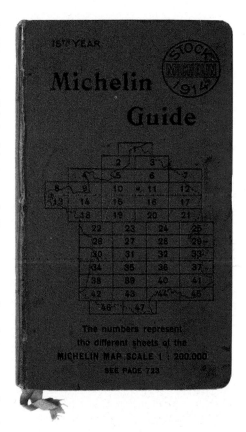

Above: The first Michelin Red Guide to France dates back to 1900. Until the 1920s they were given away free to motorists.

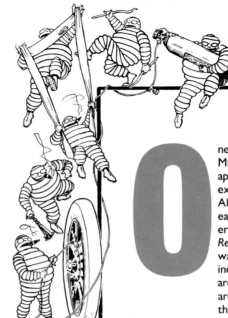

Below: This photograph, of 15 September 1910, taken from Sloane Avenue, shows the building under construction. The walls have been completed to roof level and the construction of the ferro-concrete hollow roofing was in progress. The Burmantofts ceramic panels of interlocking tyres and 'M' motif are already in position.

Opposite: Progress diagram of the building from Mouchel-Hennebique Ferro-Concrete.

One of the most innovative features of Michelin House is perhaps the least visually apparent: it is one of the finest early examples of a concrete building in Britain. Although Michelin House was one of the earlier buildings to employ this new material the fact that one English text book, *Reinforced Concrete* by Marsh and Dunn, was already into its third edition by 1904 indicates that the material had already aroused considerable interest among architects, engineers and builders, even though it had not actually been employed.

Just as the motoring press of the time expounded its aesthetic and functional merits, it was well documented in technical publications for its structural qualities. The monthly *Ferro-Concrete Journal* of September 1912 states that:

> In the original portion of the building, completed in December, 1910, the ferro-concrete work comprises wall and interior columns, wall lintels, floor and roof beams, solid and hollow monolithic flooring and roofing, and similar work over the boiler house, coal store, and other parts of the basement under the motor garage and yard.

The article goes on to give a detailed and illustrated description of the construction schedule, concluding that:

> The complete erection of the Michelin Building in the record time of five months is a convincing proof of the rapid construction rendered possible by ferro-concrete.

The consulting engineers responsible for the structural design of Michelin House were Messrs. L. G. Mouchel and Partners, the sole agents for Hennebique ferro-concrete in the United Kingdom. Hennebique's ferro-concrete system offered clear open spaces (it is this quality that has made the Michelin Building so uniquely suitable for conversion today into contemporary office and retail usage). The construction speed and fire resistant properties also offered by the system must have been particularly important to the Michelin brothers, not least for storage of such quantities of inflammable material. (Fire resistant glazing, too, was emphasised on Espinasse's drawings.) It was possible to build a reinforced concrete skeleton, complete with floors and staircases, in as little time as was needed for erecting just the steel frame of a conventional building because, as explained in the company handbook *Mouchel-Hennebique Ferro-Concrete*:

> *In the first place, the constituents of Ferro-concrete can be obtained far more freely in all parts of the country, and unlike stone, timber and steel do not involve special preparation in workshops before delivery. In the second place, the method of construction is one favouring rapidity, inasmuch as the materials can be handled with great readiness by mechanical plant and a minimum amount of manual labour.[1]*

1. *Mouchel-Hennebique Ferro-Concrete*, London, 4th Edition, p. 27

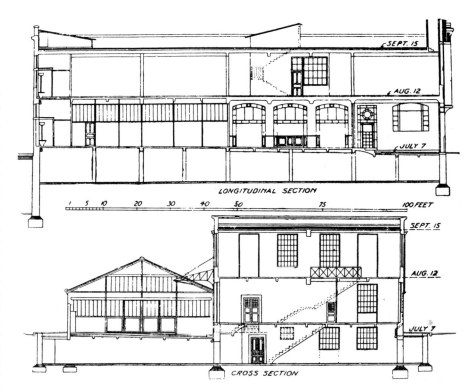

LONGITUDINAL SECTION

CROSS SECTION

The speed with which the building was constructed is illustrated in the process diagrams and in four photographs.

Mouchel and Partners had been responsible for the Liver Building in 1910, a seventeen storey granite-clad building in Renaissance style, which at that time was the tallest concrete building in Europe. Their treatment of the Michelin Building was extremely thorough and a complete set of drawings showing the construction of the building is still in existence at Mouchel's offices today.

Mouchel himself had patented the floor design, which utilised a special hollow-block concrete construction reinforced with steel rods to give exceptional lightness and strength.

Another advantage of the reinforced structure was that the building could be extended upwards, without any alteration to the lower floors, an important feature in a building designed to accommodate later additions, so that the ceiling of the first floor was able to become the floor of the second floor when the building was extended in 1912. Although the structure was not visually expressed and load-bearing brick was still employed in the walls, it represented, in 1911, the most radical departure from convention afforded by the building.

Below: Michelin's office at 97 boulevard Péreire, Paris. Built in 1908 this is the only other building known to have been designed by François Espinasse. A more functional design than the British headquarters, it was however decorated with a similar set of tiled panels; the image of Bibendum showing the 'Semelle' sole of his boot is also duplicated, but this earlier version is rendered in tiles rather than stained glass.

f the resplendently opulent (some woul say vulgar) French *dix-huitième* style of th RAC Club, Pall Mall, (1908-11) by Charle Mewès and his young English partner, A. Davis, epitomises the social acme of Edwar dian motoring's heyday, then the contem porary, strikingly tile-clad 'modern' Frencl exuberance of François Espinasse's Micheli Tyre Company Fulham Road building pro vides its most original commercial expres sion in Britain. In their individual ways these two temples of the nascent moto age perfectly convey the glamour o France's early predominance in the de velopment of the motor car.

The Michelin brothers made their reputa tion in the 1890s through their successfu adaption of the pneumatic bicycle tyre to the motor car. By 1908, with a rapidly expanding industrial base at Clermont-Ferrand, they had built themselves presti gious headquarters in Paris. The Michelin brothers, however, were not only astute businessmen but brilliant publicists as well. Both had trained at the Beaux-Arts school, Edouard as a painter and André as an architect, and no doubt they closely super-vised François Espinasse – one of their engineers from Clermont-Ferrand – who was responsible for the design of the new Paris building. In 1910, the brothers com-missioned a set of decorative tiled panels, based on cartoons by Ernest Montaut, depicting the racing successes achieved with Michelin tyres. They were made by Gilardoni Fils et Cie of the rue du Paradis, Paris, (The rue du Paradis was and remains a centre of the ceramic and glass trade in Paris and is architecturally most strikingly

ersonified by no. 18, now the Musée de 'Affiche, a flamboyantly eclectic ceramic açade of 1889 by G. Jacotin and E. Brunnaus, which originally promoted the wares of the Faiencerie de Choisy.)

The Gilardoni panels were displayed on the açades of the 1908 Michelin headquarters building (and have since been reset on the present Michelin offices in the Avenue de Breteuil, Paris). It is a virtually identical set of these lively ceramic *hommages* to the glamour and speed of motoring in general — and to Michelin tyres in particular — that forms one of the most distinctive features of the Fulham Road building, where they were installed shortly before it opened in January 1911.

To pursue the comparative 'French Connection' between the RAC Club and Michelin House in London, both buildings — beneath their very different exteriors — made appropriate use of the latest French structural engineering techniques. Mewès and Davis's palatial Portland stone elevations and 'Louis XV-XVI' interiors in Pall Mall provided a fashionable veneer on a Gallic-Rationalist structural frame of steel and reinforced concrete (the Franco-British partners had made innovative use of a steel frame in their Ritz Hotel of 1903-6).

For the first phase of Michelin House (the 1910-11 Fulham Road end of the building), Espinasse provided a still more radical technical solution: a noteworthy early example in Britain of the Hennebique ferro-concrete construction system, which, although concealed behind the intentionally

eye-catching polychrome panache of the tile and brick external skin, does find a more functional expression in the rational articulation of the building's side elevations. Mouchel and Partners, who executed the Hennebique system under exclusive British licence, also patented in their own right the lightweight hollow concrete block floor used in the same building. The use of the system at Michelin House elicited considerable interest in the architectural and construction press of the time. The *Ferro-Concrete Journal* commented particularly on the speed of erection and economy by comparison with steel, emphasing the material's fire-resistant properties (a major consideration in view of London's stringent fire regulations).

In Britain sporadic experiments had been made in the use of unreinforced in situ concrete from the mid-nineteeth century: for example, G. E. Street's school houses for Marlborough College, of 1870-72, or Sway Tower Folly, Hampshire, of the 1870s, built to designs by a retired judge named Peterson. Structural metalwork had, of course, been used widely from the turn of the eighteenth century, the Crystal Palace being generally accepted as the outstanding example. Use was made of concrete and of steel between 1900 and 1910 — notably, though unexpectedly, by various of the Arts and Crafts architects, among them Lethaby, for his 1901 Brockhampton Church, Voysey's 1902 Sanderson factory and James Salmon & John Gaff Gillespie, who used a concrete-clad steel frame for their Lion Chambers office block in Hope Street, Glasgow, of 1905-6. But

the most consistent and advanced application of ferro-concrete construction in roof and floor slabs was represented by the houses, offices and schools designed by Edgar Wood and J. H. Sellars and built principally in the Manchester area between 1907-10.

Nevertheless, ferro-concrete construction remained a rarity in Britain at the beginning of the twentieth century, used only in a handful of warehouse and factory buildings. The application of the Hennebique structural frame system at Michelin House therefore stands out as an exceptional example of pre-First World War ferro-concrete construction in London.

Until the mid-nineteenth century, France's industrial development had lagged behind Britain, despite numerous novel experiments in iron and concrete construction. But by the time of the 1889 Paris exhibition it was forging ahead, as symbolised by the Eiffel tower and Dutert & Contamin's *Galerie des Machines*. A spate of ferro-concrete patent construction systems appeared in the 1880s and early 1890s, the most commercially successful being those developed by Contamin (the engineer for Anatole de Baudot's innovative ferro-cement framed Saint Jean de Montmartre church of 1897-1904), Edmond Coignet and François Hennebique.

A government commission was set up to investigate these various systems in 1892, but did not report until 1906. One of the claims made for ferro-concrete construction was its fire-resistant properties, a

factor which no doubt stimulated its popularity following the disastrous Charity Bazaar fire, which killed 137 and injured 250 of the Parisian *beau monde* in 1897.

Hennebique devised his first concrete floor slab reinforced with round-section steels in 1880. But it was the efficient simplicity of his integral reinforced concrete post and beam system, using top and bottom steel reinforcement bars linked with tie-rods, as patented in 1892 (and applied at the Barrois mill, Lille, 1896) which, combined with his business acumen, established his reputation in France and abroad. Between 1892 and 1908, he set up forty-two international licensing agencies for this system in the United States, Russia, South America and elsewhere; by 1908, 7,205 buildings had been constructed using this method.

Structural expression and its relation to purpose had long been a major preoccupation of French Rationalist architects, whether employing traditional or innovative materials. Exposed iron structural frames with polychrome brick infill panels had been used for commercial and industrial building from the late 1860s onwards. The same approach was being adopted for institutional buildings – notably schools and low-cost housing – by the late 1880s. Stone, iron, ceramics and glass were being similarly employed in the new large department stores of the same period.

In parallel with this frank expression of structure and materials, Academic architects in France during the last two decades of the nineteenth century did not balk at using concealed metal frames to

upport their eclectic classical façades. The Rationalist and Academic approaches were used to some extent with the brief flowering of Art Nouveau, when structural expression was pushed to such extremes as to be constructionally feasible only as a veneer, supported on a partially or wholly concealed structure. That ceramic tiles lent themselves as a suitable facing material for this purpose was strikingly demonstrated by Guimard in the premises for the ceramicist Coillot at Lilles of 1898-1900. The most celebrated Master Ceramicist to colaborate with Art Nouveau architects was Alexandre Bigot, who worked in Paris with Jules Lavirotte at the Hotel Ceramic of 1904, in the Avenue Wagram, and with Frantz Jourdain on La Samaritaine of 1905-10.

Initially, concrete structural frames were used much as if they were steel, but the material's potential for cantilever, elevational modelling and so on was soon exploited. With the falling from favour of Art Nouveau extremes, a plainer, more rationally controlled form of surface patterning for ceramic tile facing of the structural frame was rapidly adopted by avant-garde architects in France, such as Auguste Perret (the block of flats he designed for 25, rue Franklin, Paris, built in 1903-4), ceramicist Bigot, Adolphe Bocage (commercial premises at 6 rue du Hanovre, Paris, of 1908), Henri Sauvage (block of flats at the rue Vavin, Paris, of 1909-12), or André Arfvidson (studios at rue Campagne Premier, Paris, of 1911) Bigot ceramicist.

Despite its innovative Hennebique ferro-concrete frame, Michelin House's decora-tive tilework does not pretend to this refined austerity. The rumbustious use of geometric patterns, overt product symbolism (tyres or 'Bibendum' globes), pictorial imagery (in ceramic tiles and in stained glass) and bold graphics has obvious affinities with the brash French consumer interpretation of Art Nouveau, which, with all its unselfconscious vitality, was already acquiring distinctly Deco features. Or, seen from the other side of the Channel, Michelin House with its Burmantofts' 'Marmo' tiles, of the kind then just used on Debenham's Wigmore Street store, and its lively polychromy are in the same tradition as the British school of tile and terracotta cladding of eclectic or Arts and Crafts derivation favoured for commercial premises, pubs and theatres in the late Victorian and Edwardian decades – a tradition epito-mised by Doulton's pictorial and decorative ceramic ware, as so dramatically displayed on their 1876 showroom and headquarters (of which only the former library survives, in Black Prince Road, Kennington). And, of course, Michelin House is none the worse for that. After all, the vast terracotta pile of Harrods loomed up in nearby Knightsbridge at the same period (1900-11) and, in any case, in the then soot laden atmosphere of London the 'self-cleaning' properties of ceramic cladding had obvious practical advantages. Ironically, the 'modern' Frenchness of Michelin House was, in fact, more at home in the colourful terracotta, ceramic and brick variety of Edwardian London than it would have been in the regulated monochrome homogeneity of central Paris – if not Lille or Nancy – at this date.

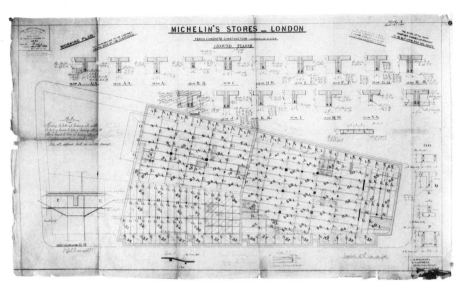

MICHELIN'S STORES — LONDON
FERRO CONCRETE CONSTRUCTION
GROUND FLOOR

WORKING PLAN

Above: One of the complete set of original construction drawings for the building that are still held by L.G. Mouchel and Partners.
Opposite: 'Michelin Building as Recently Extended'; an illustration dating from September 1912.

ven before the Michelin Building was completed, the company were discussing its first extension. They were concerned about the length of time that it took to repair a tyre in London, compared with Paris, and at a board meeting in 1910 it was agreed that the provision of a repair workshop would be looked into.

Espinasse had identified the space at the rear of his 1909 plans as being 'reserved space for future extensions' and in July and October 1911 he drew up a series of new plans and elevations for the first extension to the building. A board meeting in November 1911 approved the plans and it was agreed that additional office space as well as space for a repair workshop should be provided. The first extension, which was completed in 1912, developed the reserved area into a three and four storey extension

fronting on to Ixworth Place and Luca Place. It also added a third storey on to th rear part of the building on the Lucan Plac side. This extension is most clearly show in an illustration to an article in 'Rap Building in Ferro-Concrete' of Septembe 1912 (Vol 4, No. 3).

Ten years later the original pitch-roofe garage, which always had a rathe haphazard and temporary appearance, wa demolished and replaced by a four store extension in line with that of 1912. Th second extension was necessary to provid more offices for the still rapidly expandin company. As with the original buildin; Mouchel and Partners supervised th construction of the extension, but th work was actually carried out by Messr: W.J. Fryer & Co. of Paddington for th 1912 extension and by the Considère Cc Ltd. for the 1922 extension.

In 1927 a new factory at Stoke-on-Tren began producing the first British-made Michelin tyres and in 1930 the compan moved its head offices there. In Novembe of that year the Director's and Commercia Manager's offices and the Board Room or the first floor of the Fulham Road buildin; were converted into a caretaker's kitchen living room, and bedroom and, whils Michelin continued to use space in th basement and the ground floor, over two thirds of the building was left unoccupied Between 1933 and 1940 the upper storey; were let and used as a furniture warehouse a workshop for needlework ki: manufacturers, and as offices for the Ai Ministry.

In 1940 Michelin, concerned about the risk of bombing, removed the three Bibendum stained glass windows and sent them to Stoke-on-Trent carefully wrapped in hessian and packed in wooden crates. At the end of the war Michelin's commercial headquarters returned to London, but the reduced numbers of staff allowed them to occupy only the front and earliest part of the building and to continue to lease the remainder. The Air Ministry remained as tenants for a time and in April 1950 Foster Wheeler Ltd. signed a twenty-one year lease to occupy the 1911 and 1922 extensions. In 1952 a steel construction extending Foster Wheeler's space on the third and fourth floors was added.

In 1962 both landlord and tenant began a systematic modernisation programme throughout the interior of the building. Fortunately this modernisation programme, which was in keeping with a general swing in taste in the 1960s, concentrated on the interior of the building although enquiries were made into the possibility of updating the exterior with a new cement rendered face. False ceilings were put in and the large open plan offices were compartmentalised into smaller units divided by wood panelling and narrow corridors. The caretaker's quarters were adapted into a staff restroom and bar and the Touring Office was divided into two small interviewing rooms. The mosaic floor of the entrance hall was left intact although it was covered first with thermoplastic tiles and then, in 1973, with carpet tiles. A circle was cut out of the middle to show the image of Bibendum beneath. In 1963 the grand twenty-seven

foot long wooden sales counter disappeared completely and the original wrought iron arches and screens dividing the entrance hall from the Touring Office were concealed beneath profiled plywood panelling. But the tile pictures were left for the most part in good condition and they remained on display.

In fact it is fortunate that the rear portion of the building has survived at all. In April 1969 the front and oldest part of the building was given a Grade II listing. It is surprising that, in spite of this, outline planning permission was granted to demolish all but the listed section in 1972 in order to develop a ten storey office block that would have entirely dominated its surroundings. Luckily Michelin decided to spend the money on a new factory in North America instead.

Towards the end of the 1970s they began to clean and restore the building. The 'Marmo' tiles on the outside were cleaned and the green vertical bands reset where they had been pushed forwards. Reconstructions of the original lights were made and installed in the tyre fitting bay and entrance hall and damaged wall tiling was replaced by specially made replicas. The carpet and thermoplastic tiles on the entrance hall were carefully removed and damaged areas of the mosaic replaced.

But by 1985 the Michelin Tyre Company were finding that their first British headquarters could no longer sensibly fill their office requirements. It offered inappropriate accommodation in an unnecessarily fashionable part of London. They decided to sell the building and move to more suitable premises in Harrow on the Hill.

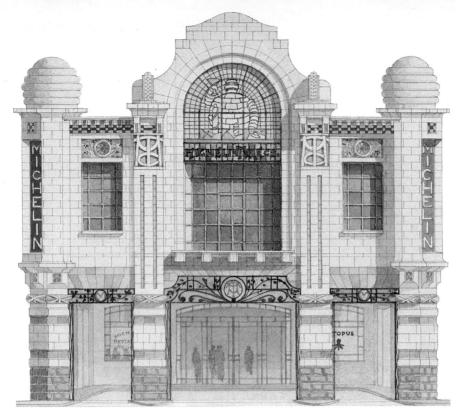

original features, such as the Bibendum stained glass windows, the enormous glass cupolas and the original wrought iron entrance gates had long since been lost. They were to be remade and reinstated and all of the tile work inside and outside the building was to be carefully cleaned and, where necessary, repaired or replaced.

In November 1985 Conran Roche and YRM made an application for planning permission, proposing that the existing floor area of 90,000 square feet should be increased to 118,000 square feet by building a new steel and glass structure to fill in the loading bay, and by adding, firstly, a neater new front end to the third floor and secondly, a new fourth floor and plant space above.

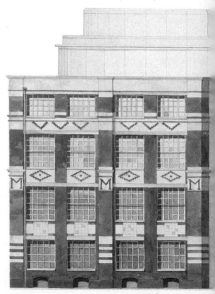

n August 1985 the Michelin Building was bought by Sir Terence Conran and Paul Hamlyn and plans were set in motion to create a new life for the building. Since Chelsea was no longer an ideal centre for distribution of tyres a new role in retailing was considered to be an acceptable way forward for the building.

The New Michelin House was to comprise a major store in the ground floor and basement, with a restaurant linked to a small oyster bar in the original Touring Office on the first floor. The remainder of the building was to continue as office space. It was also agreed that the listed front part of the building should be meticulously restored and given a new public availability. The restoration of the building, both inside and out, was to be an important aspect of its new future. Many of its most prominent

These vertical extensions were to be inconspicuous from the street and were to add a new and resolved roof line to what had become a rather bitty series of additions.

It was agreed that if the Michelin Building was to receive the sort of care and attention that it needed and deserved then some change of use was appropriate given the changes and developments that had taken place in its direct environment. It was now a famous building in one of the most desirable areas of London.

The application for planning permission was approved in January 1986 and work on the structure and the restoration of the building was begun shortly afterwards.

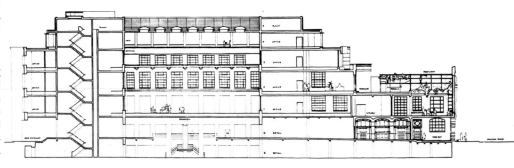

Opposite: Watercolour of the new front façade of the building by Conran Roche January 1986.

Above: Conran Roche's section through the building of October 1985, showing the Octopus Group's offices as well as the Bibendum restaurant.
Below: Watercolour, showing the new Sloane Avenue elevation with the glass infill, which formed part of Conran Roche's planning application in November 1985.

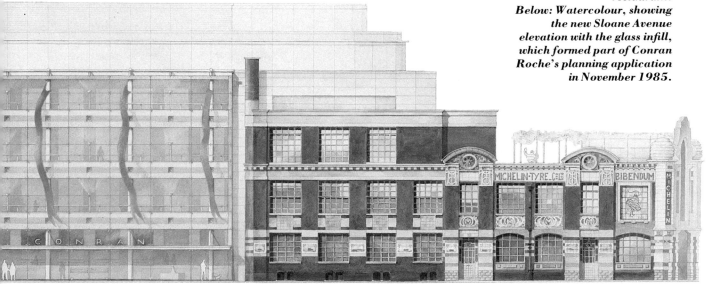

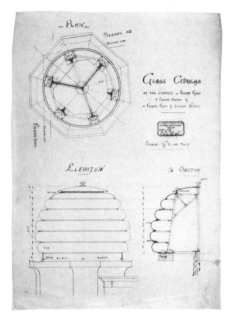

It was very difficult to find a company who would even attempt to remake the large glass cupolas (right). In the event the structure that was agreed upon correlated very closely with Espinasse's original drawing of 18 July 1910 (above).

Y RM Architects and Planners and Conran Roche were responsible for restoring the front part of the building to English Heritage's satisfaction. There were five main areas requiring attention: the stained glass windows, the cupolas, the main entrance hall and tyre fitting bay, the tiling and the wrought iron work. At the time of the sale the whole interior of the building was in generally poor condition.

Perhaps the most interesting and visually exciting area of the restoration work was the remaking of the three Bibendum stained glass windows. The originals had disappeared after being sent to Stoke for safe keeping. Their whereabouts can be traced from 1940 to 1965, but at some point in the late sixties they were removed from the basement of the administration block at Stoke; despite local radio and newspaper appeals, they were never seen again.

Very good photographs of the building taken in 1911 gave a clear picture of the cartoons for each of the windows and the closely related original publicity material provided some indication of the detailing and colours that would have been used. Since, for obvious reasons, there were no colour photographs of the original building, some artistic licence had to be allowed in the range of colours and tones. There is no record of where the originals were made, but it seems likely that they would have been of French origin. Much of the blue glass for the replicas was imported from France. The design of the cartoons was gradually refined as more detailed source material came to light and as ideas de-

veloped. The stained glass makers suggested putting circular studs into Bibendum's 'Semelle' sole. Although this probably was not on the original, it was agreed that it would be a successful and inspired departure and, after consultations with English Heritage, the idea was approved.

Lighting the stained glass proved to be one of the most difficult areas because the three windows are perhaps the most dominant features in the restaurant and so need to be read, to some extent at least, from inside as well as outside the building, at daytime and at night. Espinasse's original drawings, although excessively informative in almost every other respect, did not throw any light on this problem, but after considerable experiment a solution was found.

The domed glass cupolas which originally topped the corner turrets on the front of the building also required technical reinvention. Again, the originals had disappeared, but fortunately Espinasse had left a detailed drawing for their construction. Nevertheless, YRM had great difficulty in finding anybody who would say that they could make them. They talked to manufacturers of lighting equipment and chandeliers, and to glass blowers, and eventually they found a very old established company, experienced in a wide range of processes concerned with glass, who were prepared to submit a tender. At the same time they investigated making the domed cupolas of a plastic or fibre-glass material, but this proved impractical, not least because the cupolas were illuminated from inside. A proposal for a double curved piece of glass,

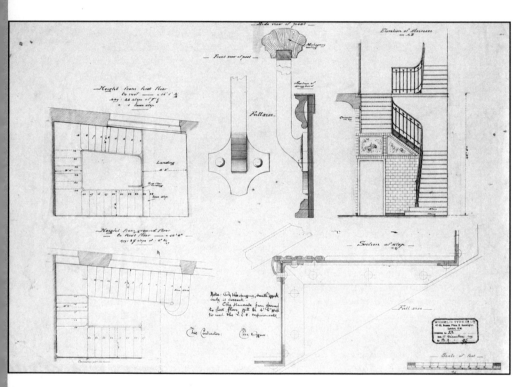

Above: Espinasse's drawing of the Details of Staircase, 1 December 1909. Until the plaster board panelling and floor covering were removed nobody realised the staircase was fully tiled.

sand-blasted on the inside face and held together with an aluminium framework, very close in design to Espinasse's original, was eventually accepted and it was agreed that this should be lit with a strong yellow light source to give the right colour effect.

The final glass features to be reconstructed and lit were the two vertical 'Michelin' panels on the front face of the building, which had been replaced by plastic versions at some point. By comparison with the stained glass and the cupolas these were very straightforward indeed.

Some restoration work had already been done in the entrance hall and tyre fitting bay in the late 1970s, but YRM's first job was to strip out the panelling inside the main hall to find out what original features were hidden beneath and what sort of condition they were in. It was found that the arches and piers between the Touring Office and the entrance hall were still there and that the original tiling was still in place throughout. Fortunately the picture panels had been maintained in good condition, but many tiles had been damaged by shot-firing of fixings into them and the wall tiling in the tyre fitting bay had been replaced in its entirety with reproduction tiles that did not match the originals precisely enough. Samples of the damaged tiles were taken off the walls and various companies were approached to try and match them exactly. They had been made inherently weak by the T-lead glaze and very light bodied clay used to give the tiles a very white appearance. The reproduction that was finally approved had a different clay body to make t stronger and the glaze was built up in thin layers to give the very light white effect. Reproductions for the egg and dart and the turquoise coloured architrave tiles were equally carefully researched. Many of the difficulties that must have been encountered in making the originals recurred in manufacturing the replicas.

The staircase to the right of the entrance hall was entirely panelled in plaster board when the building was surveyed and its renovation was not at first thought to be a high priority. However, some exploratory work was done with the idea that there might be picture tiles beneath the panelling, and it was found that the entire staircase area was not only tiled to the same standard as the entrance hall, but also complete with its own mosaic floor. The metal staircase itself is quite unique, with complex bends built up in sections that show a high degree of ingenuity and craftsmanship. After considerable discussion it was agreed that this area must also be extensively restored, with replacement tiles where appropriate. The staircase was also repainted and decorated.

The whole of the exterior was carefully cleaned and the silicon layer removed from the brickwork at the rear. There were particular problems caused by weather-damage. The tiled picture panels were in their final stages of deterioration in spite of attempts to protect them. Corners of the panels were defoliating and water was getting in and freezing, with the result that little bits of the glaze were flaking off. Had they not been restored at this point they

would have been lost. After consultation with the Victoria and Albert Museum a specialist company was called in to suggest a course of renovation and a programme involving the minimum interference with the appearance of the pictures and the maximum stabilising effect was begun.

The faience work on the outside of the building also proved difficult to repair. In parts it was so weather-damaged that it was in danger of actually falling off the building; here the blocks had to be literally cut out and replacements fixed back into position. But, again, the production of matching replicas proved to be very difficult and, wherever possible, the blocks were repaired using a pigmented resin. In order to stop the repair work discolouring in the sunshine, as had happened with previous repairs, a special coating was developed to make the pigment less sensitive to ultraviolet light.

More fortunately the decorative three-dimensional faience blocks under the eaves of the roof were all in good condition and when these were cleaned with bristle brushes and mild detergent their original colours were brilliantly restored.

Over the years many of the original windows on the building had been replaced and needed to be reinstated to their original design to give a consistent quality around the building. The screens in the main hall were also remade and the doors from the tyre fitting bay on to Sloane Avenue and Lucan Place were restored. In some places the change of use of the building made it

necessary to alter certain doors and windows in order to accommodate the increased flow of traffic and fire regulations, but in these instances the designs were made to correlate as closely as possible with the originals.

The original wrought iron gates across the front of the building had been replaced by a more modern design. English Heritage insisted that the original full lattice work design, which rolled on a bottom track, be remade and reinstated. The modern panel behind the decorative iron work above the gates was also removed, restoring the front of the building to its authentic appearance.

Inside the tyre fitting bay the tiled floor was repaired where necessary and a brass strip set in to mark the position of the weighbridge. In fact the weighbridge could have been returned to working order quite easily, but this was felt to be inappropriate as no cars were anticipated inside the newly restored entrance. The mosaic floor in the adjoining hall was also repaired; Mr Bibendum continues to raise his glass not only to Michelin tyres but also to a new future for Michelin House.

Below: Details of Mouchel's holopot floors exposed during the new construction work.

Right: The new additions to the roof of the building photographed under construction in May 1987.

Just as the Michelin Building was originally constructed from the most modern materials available, so the new addition to Michelin House — the infill slotting into the loading bay area and the additional floors accommodating the increased offices and retail space — employ some of the latest technology. Structurally, these additions were to provide a substantial challenge to all of the parties involved.

The original Hennebique ferro-concrete system with load-bearing brick walls and reinforced concrete frame was still able to support the loads for which it was designed. But the approved extensions to the build-

ing involved an increase in floor area of 30%. An increase on this scale had to incorporate its own structural support making necessary a new steel structure threading through the existing building down to the new foundations. Steel was chosen because its lightness allowed the minimum impact on the original structure and the table-like structure carrying the new floors was designed with supports around the perimeter of the wedge-shaped site to give as little intrusion into internal spaces as possible. But more complex solutions were to be solved where the new cores had to cut through the floors; here steel columns were threaded through small holes in the concrete floor slabs. Steel beams were erected under each floor to support the existing concrete, allowing the floors to be cut away at each core.

Because the earlier part of the Michelin Building was built up in a variety of structural systems the ribs in Mouchel's floors do not always line up from level to level. Each variation caused a fresh specific problem in the location of the new steel columns by the team of engineers and builders, and these and the irregular shape of the building caused the structural engineers and the steel sub-contractor to make over 1300 drawings to explain and work out construction details.

In spite of the complexity and inherent difficulties of the job, they were overcome and the restoration was completed successfully to allow Conran Design Group and YRM Interiors to move in and begin the interior refurbishment.

Conran Design Group were responsible for the interiors of the new restaurant and bar on the ground and first floors, and for the retail area. In all three spaces they opted to retain aspects relating to the history of the building whilst introducing new themes appropriate to its change of use.

The new Conran Shop occupying the middle area of the ground floor and the major part of the basement was designed to enhance the basic fabric of the architecture, whilst being a neutral backdrop to the shop merchandise. Simplicity and a 'clean line' were combined with an attempt to emulate the elegance of the building. Materials such as oak boarding, cream coloured ceramic tiles and marble in the front entrance, were selected for a quality of finish which would be enhanced by wear and ageing. The store

is divided to give the impression of differen[t] rooms, but the effect is not altogeth[er] domestic: it holds on to the feeling [of] vintage cars and luxury showrooms. Th[e] lighting throughout is felt rather than see[n] and the overall emphasis is on subt[le] and discreet design.

From the street the new glass face drop[s] straight down to the pavement, adding [a] drama and a glittering stage-like presenc[e] to what had previously been a dead façad[e] on Sloane Avenue.

Both the bar and the restaurant refer muc[h] more directly to the building's associatio[n] with tyres and, in particular, to Bibendu[m] the Michelin man. Both are named afte[r] him, but they also take advantage of ever[y] opportunity to reflect his corpulent profil[e]

Conran Design Group's proposal for the Oyster Bar (right) and Bibendum restaurant (left), April 1987.

Rimmed Bibendum detailing can be found on the bar itself and the light fittings, the china, glass, and even the tables have been specially designed to incorporate a Bibendum bulge. Bibendum china, glass, vases and ashtrays were specially designed; Jasper Conran designed the restaurant chair covers to be changed each season so that their colours might blend with seasonal flowers.

A good deal of the character of the bar and restaurant, which are both in the front and listed part of the building, stems from their original features. These have been interpreted and developed rather than slavishly copied, so that the spaces are more identifiable with their new functions. For example, the restaurant floor continues the mosaic of the ground floor areas and this material is repeated on areas of the res-

taurant bar, but here it is combined with a zinc architrave and work surface so that a utilitarian feel of culinary cleanliness is contrasted with the interplay of rich surface textures elsewhere.

Both the restaurant and the bar have French overtones with an emphasis on quality and style. The windows on to Sloane Avenue on both floors and on to Lucan Place in the restaurant are etched with maps showing the gastronomic regions of France: one is reminded of the roll down maps in the original Touring Office and again early themes and materials are carried through and developed. The wood panelling of the Touring Office and wrought iron work of the front façade are continued into the lift area taking people up to the restaurant above.

Free-standing kiosks to sell newspapers and flowers have been designed to sit in the tyre fitting bay and, here again, aspects of the original interior of the building were complemented and reflected with underlying hints of Parisian culture and elegance.

Just as parts of the building originally accessible to the public have been retained and expanded it is appropriate that the early Michelin offices have become the new headquarters for the Octopus Publishing Group. Again the spaces have been transformed and extended, adding two entirely new floors of offices to the earlier structure, and the same insistence on quality and painstaking attention to detail was applied. Although the office areas are less open to the public they occupy 5,000 square metres, nearly half of the building.

*Right: The four storey atrium is
naturally lit from seven
conical roof lights.*
*Opposite: Part of the Octopus Group's
stylish office area.*

YRM Interiors were concerned that simple, comfortable and essentially modern offices that would be efficient and pleasing to work in should be provided. They were conscious that their clients, a highly creative and competitive organisation, were accustomed to working in cellular, library-like spaces and every effort was made to provide work stations within the open plan format that would offer flexibility, comfort, and quality.

Visitors reach the Octopus Group's offices through the magnificent Fulham Road entrance hall which serves all the building's occupants. The transition from this area, with its tiled panels and mosaic floor, to the modern reception room was the subject of careful consideration by YRM Interiors. Hardwood panelling was chosen for the custom-made reception desk and the surrounding walls because, as a material, it sits comfortably with the period entrance hall; at the same time however, the technique of 'pickling' before staining has modern associations and gives a good background for the book displays. The wood panelling is then echoed in etched glass windows and screen, a feature continued on internal doors throughout the Group's premises. The lobby area between the entrance hall and the reception is paved in marble mosaic, a material chosen to complement both the ceramic Bibendum mosaic and the grey carpet of the reception room.

At first floor level and above, along the Sloane Avenue elevation, a four storey atrium has been created between the new outer glass wall and the original Michelin

loading bay wall, setting a visual contrast between the old and the new. It includes a display area for the marketing and sales staff, whose open plan offices are conveniently located on the ground floor beyond the original brick façade. As these departments have frequent visitors for presentations of forthcoming titles, the five inter-connecting meeting rooms required by the Group have been located on the ground floor on the outer side of the atrium.

The quirks and irregularities of the Michelin Building presented YRM Architects with some interesting challenges. The wedge shape of the building, the fact that its floors were not repetitive in plan, and the exceptional and varying floor to ceiling heights all had to be taken into account. One of the solutions to these irregularities proved to be a deep raised floor accommodating a void between itself and the original floor level. This new floor corrected the variations in floor to ceiling heights, effectively lowered what had been rather high window sill levels, and allowed a more economical air conditioning system to be installed. All of the services, including the air conditioning, were encased within the new raised floor void and these hidden service ducts, which also accommodated power supplies, facilitated an exceptionally discreet range of office alternatives.

Located on four floors, the offices comprise a mixture of large work stations, smaller screened work stations and individual desks. The space planning was done with the aid of YRM's in-house computer-aided design and drafting system; the arrangements

allow considerable flexibility in the future development of the different companies.

In addition to these open plan areas, special facilities have been created for the picture research library and the computer room, both of which have extra fire protection, and for various dark rooms for the production departments. There is also a modest staff cafeteria capable of seating seventy people at a time.

A pale grey office furniture system was selected and a simple white false ceiling installed to give a clear plane off which light

could be reflected. The overall impression is one of light and simplicity, the modern equivalent, perhaps, of the original effect of the Michelin offices in 1911. An executive suite with a roof terrace is provided at the front of the second floor and it is regrettable that no comparison can be made between this and the office spaces that the Michelin brothers might have used when they were in London. Nevertheless, it may be said that the new Michelin Building is every bit as concerned with modernity, efficiency, quality and style today as it was when it first opened in 1911, nearly eighty years ago.

ACKNOWLEDGEMENTS

AUTHOR'S ACKNOWLEDGEMENTS

During the preparation of this book many individuals and organisations have generously given their time and assistance. I am particularly grateful to:

Ted Fuller
Alain Sonolet, Michelin Tyre Public Limited
    Company
M. Douard, Conservatoire du Pnematique
    Michelin
John Harris
Jane Preger, RIBA Drawings Collection
Steve White and Gary Griffiths, YRM Architects
Jonathan Pile and John Donolly, Conran Roche
Chris Weedon and Wendy Wood, Conran
    Design Group
Tom Schollar, F.J. Samuely & Partners
Ken Baker
Mr P.B. Richly
Penny Olson
Simon Khachadourian, Khachadourian Gallery
Mr Jordan, L.G. Mouchel and Partners
Daniel Ward, Jones Lang Wootton
Tim Evitt, Art Tile Company
National Motor Museum
Goddard & Gibbs
David Hall T.W. Ide
Richard Hurst
Geoff Gash, Bovis

Wendy Hitchmough

The publishers would like to thank the following for supplying the material which appears on the pages listed below.

Abbey House Museum 2; Conran Roche 53; Paul Hamlyn 52, 52–53; Michelin 1, 18–25, 27, 37, 43, 50, 54 left, 56; National Motor Museum 9; P.B. Richly 6, 42 below, 55, 64.

Photographic credits:

Charlotte Benton 48 left, 49 above; Bovis/John Hovell 59; Building Magazine 58; Conran Roche 20; Geremy Butler 1, 18–19, 21–25, 27, 50, 54 left, 56; Dominique Delauney 49 below; John Hovell 4–5, 31 left, 34 left, 35 above; Jones Lang Wootton 31, 34 above right; Khachadourian Gallery 11, 13, 39, 40, 41; London Transport Museum 17; Michelin 10, 12, 26, 28, 29, 33, 34 below, 35 below, 36, 38, 46, 51; L.G. Mouchel & Partners 44, 45; National Motor Museum 7 left, 8, 14, 15 above, 16, 30, 42 above; Quadrant Picture Library 15 below, 32; Arthur Sanderson & Sons Ltd (Courtesy RIBA) 48 right; The Science Museum 7 right; Eileen Tweedy 2, 6, 9, 37, 42, 43, 52–53, 55, 64; Huw Walters 54 right.

Editor: Vicky Hayward
Design concept: Grundy & Northedge Designers
Art director: Karen Bowen
Picture research: Wendy Hitchmough and Nadine Bazar
Production: Michel Blake